# Travel Safely

## AT HOME AND ABROAD

## *Don't Be A Target!*

R. W. Worring • W. S. Hibbard • S. Schroeder

W9-DCI-251

*1996*

# Disciaimer

TRAVEL SAFELY is designed to provide information on how to travel safely. Its intention is educational. Its purpose is not to render legal, medical, or other professional advice. If such services are necessary, consult a competent professional.

Every effort has been made to make this manual as complete and accurate as possible, yet it is not a definitive text, but only a guide. The safety suggestions contained herein are believed to be accurate and will assist travelers. However, each traveler must make individual decisions and assume responsibility for their own behavior and safety.

The authors and publisher shall have neither liability or responsibility to any person or entity with respect to any loss or damage caused or alleged to be caused directly or indirectly by the information contained in this book. The authors and publisher cannot be held responsible for the results of one's actions whether or not one follows the suggestions or relies on the information in this book.

Library of Congress
Catalogue Card Number: 95-62066
ISBN: 0-940659-10-7

Printed in the United States of America

First Edition, January 1987
Second Edition, October 1987
Third Printing, Revised, January 1989
Fourth Printing, Revised, March 1991
Fifth Printing, Revised, March 1992
Sixth Printing, February 1993
Seventh Printing, September 1995
Third Edition Revised, January 1996

*Uniquest Publications*
562 West Main • Helena, MT 59601 • (406) 443-3911

# Table of Contents

# *Travel:*

## The Great Adventure

The mere mention of the word "travel" brings to mind images of exotic places, different cultures and peoples, and exciting experiences. This book will help you make these images a SAFE reality. **TRAVEL SAFELY** gives you the keys for a safe and successful trip, whether for business or pleasure. Learn to prevent problems **before** they happen. Before you are victimized, plan your safety and security as well as your itinerary. **The trouble it takes to travel trouble-free is worth it!** This book will arm you (without alarming you) with the information necessary for a safe journey and teach you how **not** to be a target. **Bon voyage**!

Traveling at home and abroad, you will be in unfamiliar places, surrounded by strangers, loaded down with luggage, and carrying large amounts of money. If out of the country you may be unfamiliar with the culture, unable to speak the language, and an easy target for those waiting to separate you from your money and possessions. People travel to enjoy some time off or for business, but problems, emergencies, and uncertainties arise. Travel can be one of the most exciting and enriching of experiences, especially if you are well prepared.

Trouble cannot always be avoided. Things go awry. Luggage, tickets, and travelers checks get lost or stolen, pockets get picked, and hijackings and terrorist incidences occur. Criminals of all sorts make a profession of "working" vacation spots and plan to steal your cash, valuables, and passport. While traveling you may get ill, injured, lost, or run out of money. If traveling abroad you may unwittingly violate local laws and social customs, or be victimized in your hotel, on public transportation, on the street, or in your car.

---

*Unfortunately, most people do not think about safety until after being victimized. That's akin to locking the barn door once the horse has run away!*

---

## How Safe Is Travel?

We all know life is full of risks, and traveling is no exception. The escalation of certain crimes against travelers (e.g., terrorism in the 80's, carjacking in the '90s) has forced the traveler to carefully weigh the risks.

---

*Traveling safe at the turn of the century means traveling smarter.*

---

Simply stated, the risks of traveling are much like that of driving a car: it is always somewhat risky, but is relatively more risky if you are unskilled at driving, if road conditions are bad, or if you are not aware and alert to changing driving conditions. Following this analogy, the amount of travel risk you may face depends on what you know about traveling safely, where you go, and who you are. Risks become much greater if you are an executive of a multi-national corporation in a third world country. According to "A Survey of Corporate Programs for Managing Terrorist Threats"

6

by Professor Harvey, "if recent trends of the past are any indication of the future strategies of terrorists, United States Multi-National Corporations will continue to be their primary targets." The fact that most terrorists acts are successful (87% of attempted bombings go off as planned, 76% of hostage taking attempts work, and 75% of all assassination attempts are successful) justifies the concerns of corporate leaders for the safety of corporate assets and personnel throughout the world. **On the other hand, if you are not a traveling executive** then other problems are more likely to occur than a terrorist incident. For example, you are more likely to become a victim of assault, rape, or robbery (escalating at 40% per year in such areas as Dade County, Florida), or the latest road hazard for travelers, "carjacking", the violent and sometimes deadly offspring of auto theft occurring at the rate of 70 per day in the United States alone. Also the broadening of crime targets once thought to be safe (schools, malls, restaurants, homes, courtrooms, the workplace and ATM stations) has more travelers feeling vulnerable.

*Statistically, you are more likely to drown in your own bathtub than fall victim to a terrorist.*

The average traveler is far more likely to suffer loss or theft of his money, valuables, and property, or have medical, legal, transportation, and accommodation problems, than becoming a victim of violence. Yet, it is the horror stories, and not the statistics that we most remember. And the fact remains that it **can** happen to you! Going places whether to work, on business or vacationing has always meant enjoying the freedom of the open road and still being able to keep out of harm's way. Unfortunately, this has become more difficult.

There is no absolute defense against criminal activity and the risks inherent in travel, but the development of a personal safety travel plan composed of reasonable and prudent precautionary measures will significantly **reduce** those risks.

## How to Use this Book

**TRAVEL SAFELY** will help make your travel even safer. It will prepare you to recognize, prevent or avoid, and deal with a wide variety of personal security-related situations, concerns, and problems. Whether you are traveling for pleasure or business, at home or abroad, it will give you a good basic knowledge of security so that you can enjoy your travels and return safely. **TRAVEL SAFELY** will take you all the way from securing your home before you leave, through the gauntlet of possible perils and hazards waiting for you on your trip, to returning safely home through Customs.

**TRAVEL SAFELY** will teach you to travel **smarter** by helping you develop a total personal protection plan.

*The purpose of TRAVEL SAFELY is to help you develop a "safety awareness" and provide you with the necessary practical information for trouble-free travel at home and abroad.*

This book is conveniently arranged by major subject areas for easy reference. It is recommended, however, that you read the entire book in preparation for the unexpected. As with learning any new skill or behavior, you should periodically review the material in **TRAVEL SAFELY** so that you will respond appropriately and automatically when needed. Safety suggestions for "home" and "abroad" are intermixed, since many apply to each. For easy reference there is an index at the back of the book for different subject areas.

## Know the Risks

Accustomed to ordinary life, few travelers even think of encountering trouble when traveling. They may rightfully ask: "What should I be concerned about?" Away from the protective network of home and a familiar environment, a traveler runs the risk of encountering any situation. **To be forewarned is to be forearmed**.

The following list identifies some of the safety concerns, hazards, and perils that a traveler may face at home or abroad:

**Travel Hazards**
- Damaged or lost baggage; lost or stolen passports, credit cards, cash, travelers checks, tickets
- Cancellations, over-booking, lost reservations
- Getting lost, accidents, e.g., traffic, airplane
- Dangerous transportation & accommodations, e.g., motel/hotel fires
- Civil unrest, war, terrorism, e.g., hijackings
- Unstable or unfriendly governments & organizations
- Violation of local laws and social customs
- Corrupt foreign law enforcement

**Criminal Activity**
- Crimes against property: burglary, theft, auto theft
- Crimes against persons: robbery, kidnap, assault, rape, murder

**Medical Hazards**
- Heart attack, broken limbs, trauma
- Exposure to contagious disease, infections
- Food poisoning, dysentery, allergy reactions
- Radiation poisoning
- Inadequate medical facilities and personnel
- Mental/emotional stress

**Environmental/Ecological Hazards**
- Contaminated water or food, exotic parasites
- Toxic wastes, oil spills, toxic smog

- Disease bearing insects, epidemics
- Poisonous snakes, spiders & plants
- Nuclear accidents

**Natural Catastrophes**
- Floods, fires, lightning
- Hurricanes, typhoons, hail, blizzards, tidal waves
- Avalanches, rock slides, earthquakes, volcanoes

This list is not all-inclusive, but can be used as a guide to help assess the level of risk inherent in traveling to any designated geographical area. Many of these risks are beyond your possible control, and others are of such a remote possibility of occurrence, that you should not allow them to hinder your travel desires. Many of the risks, however, are of a sufficient frequency, and are within your ability to prevent or mitigate, that you should seriously plan for them. **TRAVEL SAFELY** will help prepare you to do this.

---

*Risk is part of everything we do.*

---

**Acceptable Risks**

The intelligent and prepared traveler tries to assess the level of acceptable risk, as the vacation or business trip you save may be your own. In some cases the life you save may be your own.

**To assess the level of acceptable risk:**
  (a) select the geographical area to be visited;
  (b) learn the perils and hazards potentially applicable to the designated area;
  (c) evaluate the probability and frequency of them occurring;
  (d) assess your ability and willingness to cope with the possible risks; see page 63 for the *Safety Scan Exercise*, and page 116 for information regarding travel in high-risk areas abroad.
  (e) make a "Go" or "No Go" decision;
  (f) if "Go", prepare as best as possible for your trip by studying **TRAVEL SAFELY.**

# "Know Thyself"

It all begins before you actually leave on your trip. Without proper planning and preparedness you are inviting trouble. You will need certain skills and resources to make your trip a safe one. Some of these you already possess; others you will have to develop.

**To travel prepared, you must begin by "knowing thyself."** Your personal likes and dislikes, expectations, tolerance for frustration, ability to adapt, and temperament, will all drastically influence your travel experience. Honest self-reflection, evaluation, and subsequent modification will help you to develop a proper mental set to get the most out of your travels, and to help you travel safely.

*Don't leave home without being prepared.*

## Prepare Your Attitude

The first phase of preparedness should be to assess and develop the proper awareness and skills necessary for your personal protection. Ask yourself such questions as:

- "Am I aware of potentially dangerous situations in which I may find myself? Do I know how to prevent them?"
- "Do I know how to respond in certain dangerous situations?"
- "Am I easily upset by delays, changes in plans, bad weather? Am I able to adapt to these adverse conditions, or do I tend to make a bad situation worse by escalating it to a disaster? What if I can't speak the language?"
- "Am I irritated by rules and procedures?"
- "Am I mentally alert and physically fit?"
- "Do I let people take advantage of or intimidate me?"
- "Do I enjoy new experiences and new people?"

- "How dependent am I on my physical comforts and habits? How frustrating will it be for me if I'm unable to brush my teeth due to contaminated water? What if my room has no shower? What if I can't sleep at my usual time, or if it's too cold, hot, humid, or noisy to sleep?"

- "Can I tolerate or even enjoy radical changes in diet? What if I can't get anything to eat that I'm accustomed to?"

## Mental Tactics for Staying Trouble-Free

**Plan**. Research your destination and make thorough travel plans. The more you learn the less likely you are to incur any difficulties while traveling. Travel information is plentiful. Review the travel sections of major newspapers and magazines (e.g., *Travel & Leisure, Travel-Holiday* ). Read good travel guidebooks like **Fielding's, Fodor's** and **Frommer's**. Public libraries and bookstores usually have travel sections. Write the national tourist bureaus of the countries you plan to visit for general information. For up-to-date travel information abroad, write the U.S. Embassy or Consulate in the countries you plan to visit. Their addresses and phone numbers are listed in Washington, D.C. phone directories and in the *Congressional Directory*, which are available in most libraries. *Foreign Offices in the U.S.* lists the addresses of foreign diplomatic offices.

**Learn coping strategies.** "Mental rehearsal" and "guided imagery" are helpful techniques for learning how you might cope with certain situations, and for teaching yourself new responses. For example, imagine yourself confronted by a mugger. How do you respond? How would you **want** to respond? Now imagine yourself responding in this desired manner. If repeated several times you are reinforcing a new behavior, one designed to help you stay out of trouble.

**Develop a "natural warning system."** It is now well known that humans, like animals, have a tremendous (but suppressed) instinct for self-preservation, an intuitive or sixth sense for detecting and avoiding danger. Learn to listen to your inner awareness. A deep-seated uneasiness may sound an alarm, even though everything around you may seem normal.

**Expect the best.** True to the principles of "self-fulfilling prophecy", travelers who constantly expect the worst will probably get it.

**Develop a secure "presence."** Act self-assured, and don't appear weak, lost, or give off clues of being vulnerable. Stay in control of your body language, voice, and activities. Practice before you leave on your trip. Don't look or act like a victim (some authorities believe that victims send subtle "magnetic" messages to their attackers). You don't need to look tough, just confident.

- Don't underestimate the possible dangers, but don't be paranoid.
- Use your head. Be alert, relaxed, and think.
- Practice pattern interruption. Become unpredictable in your routines; vary the times, places and ways you do things.
- Develop good safety habits. Make it a habit to lock doors, check the back seat of your car before getting in, being alert to all things going on around you, etc.
- Think ahead. Anticipate. Make it an adventure!

---

*Use your senses; put your eyes and ears to work spotting danger as well as beauty.*

---

## Health & Medical Preparation

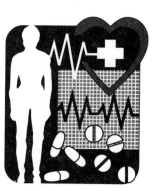

Your second level of defense after proper mental preparedness is physical preparedness. Travelers need to be attentive to their health since they are subject to added stress, increased activity, jet lag, unfamiliar infectious agents, different diet, etc. With proper forethought and preparation, most health risks can be avoided.

**Before traveling, carefully assess the state of your health:**
- Are there any health reasons why you should not travel to your chosen destination?

- Do you have a health condition that needs special care or a special diet? Will it be available on your trip?

- Will your trip require increased exercise? If so, can you handle it? If not, get in shape.

- Your personal medical information is the first thing needed for treatment following an accident or emergency - it can save your life. Carry a letter signed by your physician in a relevant language as well as English describing the state of your health and any special health problems.

**If you have a serious health condition:**

- Pre-plan in conjunction with your physician.

- Travel with a companion who is aware of your condition.

- Carry a medical summary card specifying the nature of your medical problem, medication and dosages, name and phone numbers (both home and office) of your physician, allergies to any medications or insects, blood type, notification of being a contact lens wearer, etc.

- Wear a Medic Alert tag (see *Appendix 1, Traveler Resources*, page 125).

- Get a check-up if it seems appropriate.

- Evaluate the physical demands of your proposed trip relative to your general health, e.g., can you withstand the extreme altitudes of Macchu Picchu?

- If you have a serious heart or lung condition, breathing may be difficult in airplanes (cabin pressure may be equivalent to 8,000 feet above sea level).

- Know your blood type.

- If you are older or have a chronic illness or are particularly susceptible to the flu, ask your doctor (who can check with the **Centers for Disease Control**) about outbreaks of flu, Eboli, Hantaviris or Dengue Fever in the areas you plan to visit. Or, write the Center directly in Atlanta, GA 30333, for current bulletins on disease outbreaks.

**If you are planning to travel abroad, here are some special considerations:**

- Before leaving, check with your physician about any special health or dietary considerations for your destination, e.g., eating shellfish in areas around the Mediterranean may expose you to hepatitis.

- Inquire of your physician or the **U.S. Public Health Service** of any necessary immunizations or precautions well in advance of your trip, e.g., vaccinations for cholera and yellow fever may be required. If so, get them early on in case you have an adverse reaction to the vaccine.

- Check with your travel agent or appropriate Consulate to be sure you can take your prescription drugs into the country you plan to visit.

---

*Carry your medicine in your carry-on bag in case your checked baggage is delayed or lost.*

---

- If any of your prescribed medications contain narcotics, obtain a letter from your doctor attesting to your need for them.

- Carry an adequate supply of any prescribed medications, labeled and in their original container. Carry the prescription as well (but in a different place than your medicine) in case you run out of or lose your medication. It may also be necessary at Customs. Know the generic name of any medications.

- If malaria is a problem at your destination, check with your physician about taking malaria-preventive medication.

- If you are not feeling well you are more vulnerable. So, it is important to avoid jet lag ("travel dysrhythmia"), whose symptoms include constipation, stomach cramps, headache, general malaise, and exhaustion. **Observe the following precautions:**

    ☛ Schedule an early morning flight, or at least one that

arrives at your destination relatively early.

☛ Be well rested before your flight.

☛ Exercise on the plane, elevate your legs whenever possible, both during and right after your flight. Drink lots of water, and eat moderately.

☛ Break long trips into segments by planning stop-overs.

• To recover from jet lag, allow one day to catch up for every time zone over five that you cross.

• Check your health insurance policy for overseas coverage; is it adequate or do you need additional overseas coverage?

• Medicare **does not** assume responsibility for medical bills once you leave the U.S. or its possessions, therefore, it is wise for senior citizens to look into additional travel medical insurance before leaving on a trip outside the country.

---

*Travel expands the mind but loosens the bowels, so be prepared.*

---

• You will be exposed to new allergens in foreign countries, so carry an antihistamine and eye drops if you are hyper-allergenic.

• In tropical climates drink plenty of liquids to avoid dehydration, and take precautions against sunburn.

---

*Wading in the Nile invites exotic parasitic infestations.*

---

• The World Health Organization advises travelers that: *all raw food is liable to contamination and the traveler should avoid salads and uncooked vegetables and thin-skinned fruits. Undercooked and raw meat, fish and shellfish may also carry various intestinal pathogens.*

- Unless you determine that the water is safe, drink only bottled beverages or water that has been boiled for at least 15 minutes. If the water is unsafe, don't even brush your teeth in it; if you sing in the shower, don't! And don't forget about ice cubes!

- A good diet and plenty of rest are good prevention against sickness and travel-related stress.

- An insurance policy that covers emergency medical evacuation is worth considering because if appropriate care isn't available an air ambulance will take you to a modern hospital.

- For a world directory of English-speaking doctors, recommended immunizations and medications, significant contagious diseases, and risk charts and related information about malaria and schistosomiasis, join the **International Association for Medical Assistance to Travelers (IAMAT)**.

**If you are diabetic:**
- Let a travel companion help carry some of the insulin and syringes in case yours are lost or stolen.

- Always carry a quick source of glucose in case of insulin reaction, e.g., carry some snacks.

- Many physicians recommend diabetic travelers carry a supply of glucagon for cases of extreme hypoglycemia. Speak to your doctor before you go.

- Try to keep your supply of insulin and syringes with you as checked baggage is often lost.

- Have your physician write out an extra prescription you can take with you on your trip in case of emergency. A letter describing your condition in a relevant language as well as English would be helpful as well.

# Paper Work

The world runs on paper. To travel safely out of the country you will need certain documents.

## Documents

### Passport

A passport is essential most anywhere in the world. It is the most valuable document you'll carry abroad. If you've never had a passport contact your local passport office, courthouse, or post office for application procedures. If you already have a passport, check its expiration date to see if it will be valid for the duration of your trip (if not, renew it before leaving). If you return to the U.S. on an expired passport you are subject to a passport waiver fee of $60.

- It used to be legal for a whole family to travel on one passport, but no longer. Each family member must have an individual passport.

- Check your new passport for correctness before signing it. If there are any errors, return the passport to have it corrected. Never alter or change any part of your passport as this will invalidate it.

- Always carry your passport securely on your person, e.g., in a "passport wallet". Don't pack it in your baggage.

- Never surrender your passport to anyone except authorized immigration officials or police officers and, in some countries, hotel reception clerks. Never lend your passport to anyone.

- Before leaving on your trip, make two photocopies of the front pages and write your passport number on each. Leave one copy with a friend at home, and carry the other with you (but in a separate place from your real passport). You will need this in case of theft or loss. A notarized copy of your birth certificate will also be most helpful.

- Carry two spare copies of your passport photo in case you lose your passport and need to apply for a replacement.

**Visa**

For extended stays in many countries, and for admittance to others (e.g., Eastern European, Middle Eastern, and African countries), you will need special notations and stamps known as "visas." For details, obtain **Passport Office Publication M-264**.

- Apply to the Embassies or Consulates of the countries you plan to visit, or consult your travel agent. Be sure to get the countries' latest visa requirements.

- Passport offices **cannot** help you get visas.

- Some countries will not grant visas without proof of inoculations.

- Be sure to obtain visas **before** you leave; apply far in advance of your departure date.

- Carry two extra passport photos in case you want to apply for a visa during your trip.

**Tourist Card**

Tourist Cards are a proof of citizenship and are required by a few countries, like Mexico and some South American countries.

- Obtainable at airline ticket offices, travel agencies, the country's Embassy or Consulate, or ports of entry.

- You must show proof of U.S. citizenship, either with a passport or birth certificate.

**Proof of Citizenship**

Some countries only require proof of U.S. citizenship in the form of a current or expired passport, a birth certificate, a naturalization certificate, or voter registration card. Such proof is needed to enter and depart the country.

**Medical Documents**

- Carry any prescriptions you have with you so you can replace medications lost or stolen, to obtain refills if necessary, and to avoid any hassle at Customs.

- Obtain prescriptions from your doctor for constipation,

diarrhea, insomnia, dysentery, and other common health problems.

- If any immunizations are necessary for your trip, have your doctor sign an *International Certificate of Vaccination* or "yellow card" obtainable from your local County Health Department. An increasing number of countries have established regulations regarding AID's testing. Check with the Embassy or Consulate of the country you plan to visit.

- Have your physician include a history of your vaccinations on your "yellow card" since proof of immunization may be necessary to travel through any areas with an outbreak of certain diseases.

- If you have a specific medical problem, contact **Medic Alert Foundation International**. The Foundation will provide you with a tag with an identification number, the medical information (e.g., epilepsy, diabetes, allergies to penicillin), and an emergency toll-free number.

### International Driver's License

An International Driver's License is required in most countries and can be obtained from your local chapter of the American Automobile Association if you plan to drive in a foreign country.

- Check with the Embassy or Consulate of the country in which you plan to drive for their specific requirements. For example, you would think that a U.S. driver's license would be valid in Mexico, but it's not.

### Certificate of Registration

Unless you have acceptable proof of prior possession, foreign-made personal items taken abroad are subject to duty. The purchase receipt, bill of sale, insurance policy, or jeweler's appraisal, is considered reasonable proof. Foreign-made items that you will be taking on your trip for which you do not have acceptable proof should be taken to the nearest Customs Office or port of departure (e.g., international airport, port of entry) to obtain a *certificate of registration*.

## Lost Passports & Tickets

Protect your passport with everything **but** your life!

**If your passport is lost or stolen in the United States:**
- Contact the **Passport Office**, Department of State, Washington, DC 20524, or the nearest passport agency.

**If your passport is lost or stolen abroad:**
- Notify the Passport Section of the nearest U.S. Consulate. Report it to the police, who will fill out a report (**get a copy**).

- Present this copy to the Consulate along with proof of your U.S. citizenship and identity, e.g., a driver's license, notarized copy of your birth certificate, the original number, date and place of issue, and two passport photographs.

- Apply for a replacement immediately.

**If your ticket is lost or stolen:**
- Record your airline ticket numbers, date, place of issue, flight numbers, and cost and keep separate from your tickets in case of loss. This information will facilitate reimbursement or replacement.

-----

***Treat your tickets like money as they are
easily converted to cash.***

-----

- Report any loss or theft immediately to the airline refund department and get a *lost ticket declaration*. Fill it out and send a copy to your credit card company if you used a card to purchase the ticket; your account will be credited with the amount of the ticket. The airline charges a fee for processing the claim.

- If you paid for your ticket with cash or check, you will be reimbursed only after a waiting period.

---

*If your ticket is used illegally by someone else during the waiting period, you are liable for the loss.*

---

- You also need to leave certain information with a responsible family member, see *Appendix 5, Pretravel Information for the Family*, page 133.

## Cash, Checks or Credit Cards

More than a million travelers lose cash overseas each year from theft or loss, and people get fleeced of their money everyday on the streets of America. Traveler's checks and credit cards are the preferred secure way to handle your money. If traveling abroad, bank money orders, cashier's checks, and letters of credit are usually **not** honored.

### Traveler's Checks

- After purchasing traveler's checks (available at most banks), count them to be sure none are missing, then sign them as instructed (that's your security against someone else cashing them in if lost or stolen).

- Record the check numbers on a separate sheet of paper in case of theft or loss, and leave a copy with a friend at home.

- Record the number, date, amount, and where you cash each check.

---

*Never countersign a check until the moment you cash it.*

---

- Never cash a traveler's check or exchange money except at legitimate places, i.e., dealing on the black market may get you counterfeit bills, arrested, or ripped off.

- Before you leave on your trip, ask your traveler check company for the loss reporting and replacement procedure for the cities you plan to visit (it varies depending on the company and the city).

- In case of theft or loss, report it at the nearest branch office (if there is one) of the company that issued the checks (bring your passport), and report it to the local police.

- If a loss or theft occurs on a weekend or off-hours, check the phone book for a 24-hour number (most traveler's check companies have an arrangement with car rental companies or hotel chains).

**Credit Cards**

- Take only the credit cards you may need and leave all others at home in a safe place.

- Make two photocopies (of both sides) of the credit cards you take, leaving one with family or a friend at home and taking the other with you (keep separate from the cards) which will be helpful in case of loss. Record the toll-free number to call in case of a loss, you'll find it on your recent bill, if it's not on the back of your card.

- Know your credit limit and be sure not to charge over that amount on your trip, especially when abroad.

- Verify any charges before signing and keep all slips until the billing has been received (make sure it's the correct amount).

- Check all receipts to be sure the numbers haven't been altered. In some countries, Americans have been arrested for innocently exceeding their credit limit.

- For financial emergencies, major card companies provide cash.

- Each time you use your card, make sure you get **yours** back so you don't end up with someone else's or a counterfeit card.

- In case of theft or loss, immediately report it to your card company by calling the toll-free number.
- You are liable only for the first $50 of any unauthorized charges, but prompt reporting of a loss or theft can avoid even this charge.

### Personal Checks
- Always take personal checks. Many establishments and carriers will accept them with proper identification, even overseas.

## Insurance

There are different types of insurance for different needs.

### Home Insurance
- Some policies do not cover your home if you are gone for more than thirty days; check with your agent.
- Check your policy for motel and hotel coverage.
- Does your insurance cover you for any loss or theft while abroad?

### Life Insurance
- Is your life insurance sufficient?
- Some travel agencies and clubs, and credit card companies provide additional coverage for their customers or members.
- Check to see if your life insurance has a double-indemnity clause for accidental death; it should.

### Health Insurance
- Most major health insurance companies cover their policy holders wherever they travel, but check your policy for specific language excluding expenses incurred outside the country.
- If you determine that you need additional insurance, there are companies that specialize in travel insurance .
- Carry your insurance card and the phone number of your agent.

## Baggage Insurance

- If you have a homeowner's policy, check to see if it covers your baggage. Also check to see if it covers the contents. If not, see if you can buy a *personal articles floater*, especially if taking expensive items, e.g., jewelry, camera equipment. If you buy a *floater* see if it covers new purchases made on your trip. **Trip insurance** policies are available at reasonable cost.

- Baggage insurance can be obtained from most insurance companies.

- Baggage insurance can be purchased from the airline, even at check-in time. Airlines will reimburse you for bags lost or damaged during the flight (see *Lost or Damaged Baggage* on page 37).

- Before leaving on your trip, make a list of all the items in each bag and their value. Carry a copy with you and leave one at home.

## Trip Cancellation Insurance

- Some flights have stiff cancellation charges, so someone dreamed up *trip cancellation insurance* in case you have to cancel the trip for an unforeseen reason.

## Car Insurance

- Check to see if your car insurance policy covers rented autos.

- If you plan on driving in a foreign country, does your insurance cover you and the car? Most don't!

- If you're going to be gone for a long time, put your car(s) on "storage status", i.e., comprehensive coverage only, which will save you premiums.

# *Departing*

## Secure Your Home Before Leaving

Securing your home before leaving on a trip is essential for protection of your property and for peace of mind. In most communities the police will conduct, upon request, a *security survey* of your home to advise you of vulnerable points and protective measures — follow their advice. When securing your home, do so from a thief's-eye-view.

- The fewer people you tell about your vacation or business trip, the safer your home will be.
- All doors and windows should be secured with locks. Secure all other potential entry points, e.g., pet doors, old coal chutes, cellar windows and sliding doors.
- Outside doors should be solid core or metal and locked with two devices, one being a good quality dead bolt.
- Garages are favorite entry places for burglars, so secure all garage doors and remove any tools that can be used for gaining entry to your house. If your cars are gone during your trip, cover the garage windows so burglars will not know.
- Basement windows should ideally be covered with grille or expanded metal.
- Place dowels in the track of sliding glass doors.
- If you don't have an alarm system, use alarm foil tape on the windows, and place home alarm system decals on your front and rear doors and windows.
- Similarly, a "Beware of Dog" sign may be a deterrent.
- Check with the local police to see how to participate in their **Operation Identification** program and mark your valuables

(e.g., TV, stereo, etc.) accordingly with an engraving pen (obtainable from many police departments). Record all model and serial numbers of valuables and appliances, and put **Operation Identification** stickers on your doors and windows.

- Arrange for a neighbor to watch your house, take care of the lawn or shovel the snow, pick up your newspaper (if you don't have delivery discontinued) and mail (if you don't have a mail slot), ad circulars and unexpected packages. The house should have a lived-in look.

---

*Ask your neighbor to park in your driveway.*

---

- Place several lights and a radio or TV on automatic timers.
- Don't draw all the window blinds or curtains uniformly.
- Have adequate outdoor lighting that's either on timers or in "light-control sockets".
- Your house number should be lighted and clearly visible so the police can find your house if called.
- Remove jewelry and other valuables to a safety deposit box.
- Trim tall shrubbery which blocks windows, doorways, or pathways as it provides hiding and surveillance places for burglars.
- Pay utility bills in advance so your service won't be interrupted.
- For maximum protection arrange for a trusted and responsible person to house sit.
- Give your itinerary to a trusted friend, neighbor or relative and ask him/her to call you in case of trouble. Post their name and number by the phone so the police will know who to contact in case of emergency.
- Remove your "hidden" house key. Give it to a trusted person to periodically check your house and vary the automatic timers, change the blinds and curtains, etc.

- Don't leave a ladder accessible as you automatically make your second story or roof accessible.
- Unplug your phone or set the ringer on low so anybody casing your house will not hear it ring unanswered.
- If you have an answering machine simply collect messages in the usual manner. Don't alter the message saying that you are on vacation.
- Gossip columns in small town newspapers often announce your travel plans; if unpreventable you'd better arrange for a house sitter or change your plans.

---

*Ask a neighbor to share his trash with you on pick-up days.*

---

- Don't invite burglars by taping a "Be back in two weeks" note on your door.
- Leave your most valuable and easily moveable items with a friend or neighbor, e.g., portable color television, stereo, valuable paintings.
- Inform the police of your absence and request increased patrol.
- Inventory your household furnishings and valuables and check the status of your home insurance.
- Leave some checks with a family member to pay any important bills that may come due.

## Making Safe Travel Plans

When making plans for a trip, whether for pleasure or business, it is wise to deal with travel professionals who have the experience and knowledge to help arrange a trouble-free trip. The extent of your safety plans will obviously depend upon the destination, length, and purpose of your trip.

- Shop around for a good reputable travel agency. Unless you are a sophisticated and experienced traveler who enjoys planning your own trip, a qualified agent will be an indispensable aid to planning a successful and safe trip.

- Be sure your agent carefully briefs you on all aspects of your travel, i.e., stopovers, reservations, connections.

- When planning your transportation, try to minimize the number of connections, the number of train stations, airports, lay-overs, etc. The more direct your route the more safe and secure you are.

- Check your carrier's point of origin to see if it originates from a high-risk area.

- Avoid known hot spots, e.g., do you really want to go to Beirut?

- Double-check all your tickets for errors and your reservations for accommodations.

- Ask your travel agent about any restrictions imposed by the country you plan to visit, e.g., traveler registration, currency regulations, length-of-stay limitations.

- Call the **Department of State's Overseas Citizens Service**, or any of the 13 regional U.S. passport agencies, and ask if there are any traveler advisories in effect for your destination.

- For sources of global travel conditions, turn to *Appendix 1, Traveler Resources*, page 125.

- Watch for news on any problems at your destination. Your precautions should increase in proportion to the level of political or social unrest in the area you travel to.

- Make sure all your affairs are in order (e.g., update your will if necessary, check your life insurance and leave any policies and power of attorney with your family, and organize your business) so that you are prepared for any emergency and can feel secure about leaving.

- Avoid volatile dates. Tension rises in many countries and in some areas in the U. S. during anniversaries of tragedies, e.g. Israel, on Dec. 8; India, on June 7, full moon, Mondays, etc.

- Prepare a detailed itinerary to leave with family, friends, or business in case you need to be contacted in an emergency.

- If your travel plans or return date changes (or you miss your plane!) once on your trip, notify your family.

## What to Take for Safety's Sake

What you take when traveling has a direct relationship to your preparedness and hence safety. Veteran travelers emphasize the following guidelines and suggestions for what to take on a vacation or business trip:

- Travel light! Most travelers way over do it.

- Pack only the items you need (essentials only!) and follow the multiple use philosophy, e.g., a two-sided belt, a reversible jacket, clothes that can be mixed and matched so you can make many outfits out of a few pieces.

- Inhalation of smoke and other noxious gases is one of the dangers when in a plane crash, so it is important to have a smoke hood (see *Appendix 1, Traveler Resources*, page 125).

- Go for function first, style second.

- Clothing should be appropriate for the climate of your destination; failure to do so may ruin your trip and threaten your health. Write the tourist bureau of the country you plan to visit for a free packet that includes information on climate.

- Your clothing, like your body language, should communicate confidence, strength, and action.

- Use luggage that is functional, e.g., multi-compartment soft luggage. Use smaller bags that can be managed easily if traveling alone (see *Baggage* on page 35).

- Pack and repack your bags before leaving on your trip to experiment with efficiency and to discover any unnecessary items. Even carry them around for a few days to test their manageability.

*Do not take unnecessary valuables. Use modest costume jewelry instead of the real stuff.*

- Pack toiletries and a change of clothes in your carry-on bag so you can enjoy your vacation while the airline is searching for your delayed or lost luggage!

- Put all liquids in plastic bottles, leaving enough room for expansion. In case of leakage, put the bottles in zip-lock plastic bags.

- Remove batteries from hair dryers, shavers, or other appliances in case they accidentally get turned on in your luggage.

- If you plan to use electrical appliances abroad, e.g., an electric razor, take an international adaptor and plug since currents and outlet configurations vary (see *Appendix 1, Traveler Resources*, page 125).

- Make a list of contents of each bag to carry with your other documents. In case of loss you will know exactly what's missing (and what may be missing even if your bags are returned!), which will be helpful for making an insurance claim or verifying a tax deduction.

- Carry **TRAVEL SAFELY** on your person so you can refer to it often.

## What NOT To Take for Safety's Sake

What you don't take may be as important for your safety as what you do take.

- If traveling out of the country, empty your wallet of any

identification showing military or police reserve affiliations or memberships in political groups and veteran's organizations.

- Leave obvious U.S. logos and apparel at home. Don't wear "flag" shirts if traveling to unfriendly countries or ones with hostile minorities.
- Leave your prized faded jeans and ostentatious clothing at home.
- Don't take too much cash. Don't take any valuable jewelry.
- Don't take too many clothes or bags.
- Leave your 3-day old beard at home!
- Don't take anything you can't afford to lose.

## Travel Safety Checklist

Depending somewhat on your destination, specific items to pack for your safety and survival include:

☐ all-weather clothing; depending on the climate and time of year, take clothes for warmth, rain, etc.

☐ a money belt, body or leg "safe," passport wallet, or other means of hiding and securing money, valuables, and documents

☐ take only comfortable dual purpose shoes, i.e., dressy walking shoes

☐ a waterproof and windproof jacket

☐ necessary toiletries, razor

☐ a small first-aid kit, sunscreen and chapstick

☐ Emergency Smoke Hood

☐ Pepper Spray—It is illegal to carry or pack pepper spray on board passenger planes. (Minimum $25,000 fine). Plan to purchase it at your destination.

☐ medical supplies, e.g., all prescription drugs and their prescriptions, remedies and/or prescriptions for diarrhea, constipation, motion sickness, dysentery

- [ ] a bottle and can opener
- [ ] a small waterproof flashlight with new alkaline batteries
- [ ] a walking stick, cane, or umbrella
- [ ] spare glasses or contacts and your prescription (for replacement if lost)
- [ ] if hiking, take a small lightweight knapsack or day pack
- [ ] depending on the country, take hand and laundry soap, a towel, toilet paper and disposable toilet seat covers (which you will much appreciate in countries like India)
- [ ] a compass and current maps of the areas you'll be traveling in
- [ ] emergency phone numbers, e.g., of the U.S. Consulate in the country(s) in which you'll be traveling, personal physician, family or friend back home
- [ ] notarized copy of birth certificate & two extra passport photographs
- [ ] all necessary documents, e.g., passport and visas, international driver's license, "yellow card"
- [ ] plastic water bottle and collapsible cup
- [ ] safety pins, needle and thread
- [ ] world travel alarm clock (it has a dual time display)
- [ ] lighter or waterproof matches
- [ ] small pocket mirror
- [ ] space blanket and energy snacks
- [ ] fishnet shopping bag
- [ ] nail clippers and file
- [ ] universal electrical adapter and plugs
- [ ] universal travel door lock or wedge
- [ ] water purification kit, e.g., iodine, Halazone tablets, filter
- [ ] reliable watch you can see to read at night
- [ ] bicycle cable lock
- [ ] a copy of **TRAVEL SAFELY**

Any of these items that may be questioned by airport security, e.g., your Swiss Army knife, should be packed in your checked luggage. If you only have a carry-on bag and airport security hassles you about your Swiss Army knife or another item, ask them to secure it in an envelope to give to a stewardess. If they won't, ask for an envelope and mail it home.

## Last Minute Checklist

To avoid any last minute hassles and problems:

- Reconfirm all your reservations.
- Double-check all your home security measures.
- Check all electrical appliances (is the stove turned off?) and set the thermostat low.
- Call the airport to make sure your plane is on time.
- Allow plenty of time to get to the airport and to clear airport security and Customs.

---

*Don't pack your car the night before as it's a tempting target for burglars and advertises the fact that you're leaving on a trip.*

---

- If traveling abroad obtain a *certificate of registration* from the **Customs Department** to register your valuable items (before you leave or at the airport) or else you may have to pay duty on the items upon your return to the U.S. This is especially important if you are traveling with foreign-made cameras, watches, jewelry, clothes, etc. since the customs officer will question you about purchasing them abroad. Therefore, you will need an authorized receipt to prove that you brought them with you.
- See *Appendix 5, Pretravel Information for the Family*, page 133, for important information your family needs to know while you are away or if you don't return.

# Baggage

Baggage is a whole lot of trouble, and the more you have the more trouble it is. The wise traveler travels with one carry-on soft bag, or at most, a soft bag and a garment bag. From a safety standpoint, the less baggage the less chance there is for loss (**over a million bags are lost every year!**), theft, and damage, and you are freer to move and respond quickly. The odds of arriving safe and sound and on time are much greater for you than your luggage.

- A pliable, light, durable, waterproof canvas or vinyl bag with multiple zippered compartments that will fit under an airplane seat is ideal. A shoulder strap provides the additional advantage of leaving your hands free (and is less fatiguing to carry). See *Appendix 1, Traveler Resources*, page 125  for suppliers.

- Check-in luggage should be sturdy hardcase which will resist damage to internal contents and is slash proof.

- Use covered name tags to foil the "casual" observer and, if a business person, use your business address but not your business name (don't advertise your executive status or the address of your empty home). Never use your business card for a name tag as it tells too much about you.

- Putting a sticker with your name, address and phone number on the inside of your luggage, along with your itinerary will help to reunite your luggage with you. It will also prove ownership if someone falsely claims your bags.

- Make sure the name on your bags matches the name on your ticket to expedite retrieval if they are lost.

- Remove old destination tags and stickers so your bags aren't sent to the wrong destination.

- Don't plaster your bags with stickers from fancy hotels.

- If checking bags, each bag should be locked and strapped or taped (with duck tape or strapping tape). This discourages pilfering and prevents the bags from popping open. Convenient luggage straps are carried by some travel stores (see *Appendix 1, Traveler Resources*, page 125).

> ***Even carry-on bags can be carried off by someone else.***

- Two small bags are easier to handle than one very large one.

- Don't overpack your luggage as it may pop open.

- If you must take large luggage, use those with rollers. Strap-on rollers are offered by some travel stores (see *Appendix 1, Traveler Resources*, page 125).

- Combination locks are usually better than the usual cheap and tiny key locks. Besides, master keys for brand-name luggage are available to baggage handlers, airlines, and hotel employees. Keep your bags locked since thieves are looking for the easiest marks.

- Don't use "showcase" luggage.

- Mark your bags with a distinctive colored tape for easy identification in busy baggage claim areas. This also helps avoid the problem of someone else mistaking your bags for theirs.

- Valuables, such as jewelry, cash, documents, fragile items, important medicine, expensive clothing, should be in your carry-on bag; that way they will be sure to arrive with you. Never pack anything irreplaceable in your checked bags.

*Most stolen baggage reports involve theft in and around airports, and lobbies and parking areas of hotels and motels.*

- Check with your travel agent or airline about baggage allowance on international flights and restrictions on carry-on bags.

- Arrive at the airport (dock, terminal, station) to allow plenty of time for your bags to be loaded onto the plane (ship, bus, train); most lost luggage is checked-in too close to departure time.

- If short on time, don't use the curbside baggage service, but take it directly to the check-in counter and make sure it's tagged correctly and put on the conveyor belt.

- Keep your claim check secure; you'll need it to claim your bags.

- When arriving at your hotel don't leave your bags unattended on the sidewalk to find a porter in the hotel or to register.

- If it's absolutely necessary to leave your bags unattended for awhile, cable them to a fixed object with a bicycle cable-lock (they're lightweight and easy to pack).

- If driving, leave your bags in the trunk of the car instead of the back seat, or under a blanket if in a station wagon.

## Lost or Damaged Baggage

- Report your missing baggage promptly with the carrier. If they still can't find your bags, file a written claim notice (retain a copy). You may have to wait several months to make sure it doesn't turn up before getting reimbursed.

- Your only proof that the carrier lost your bags is your claim check, so never surrender it until your bags are found. Get a receipt if the carrier insists on taking your claim check, or photocopy it.

- If a carrier loses or damages your luggage, it will compensate you for your loss up to a certain amount depending on the policies of the carrier. Additional insurance can be purchased from the carrier, but jewelry is almost never covered.

- If you use an **American Express** card to buy your ticket on a common carrier, for a minimal fee, your carry-on bags are insured by them.

- If the carrier loses your luggage, check to see if it provides emergency toilet kits or refunds to buy essentials.

- If your luggage is found, check the contents of your bags. If there is any damage or loss, immediately file a claim with the carrier (retain a copy).

---

***Overpacked bags will be disqualified from reimbursement.***

---

- Some types of items are exempt from reimbursement if damaged or lost in checked bags. The **Airline Tariff Publishing Company's** "domestic general rules" states: *The airline is not liable for the loss of, damage to or delay in delivery of valuable, fragile or perishable items, including but not limited to money; medication (prescription and nonprescription); jewelry; silverware; negotiable papers or securities; electronic, photographic or video equipment; samples; heirlooms; antiques; artifacts; works of art or other valuables included in a passenger's checked baggage…*

# *Protect Yourself*

## Executive Safety

Executives whether male or female traveling on business have more to worry about than tourists, so certain special precautions should be taken.

- Be sure family members know where to find important personal information while you are away or if you don't return. See *Appendix 5, Pretravel Information for the Family*, page 133.

- All travel arrangements should be kept restricted to a "need to know" basis.

- Secretaries should be instructed not to give out any information regarding your travel plans and all business calls should be handled by another executive.

- Inform family members of the need for keeping travel information confidential. They should tell callers that you are not available at the moment and take a message (this precaution is as much for your family's safety as your own). Your family can call you at your destination if the message is important.

- Don't discuss any travel plans with strangers.

- Travel light so you can move from place to place quickly.

- Vary your travel routes (e.g., from your hotel to office) and times of travel; criminals often keep their victims under surveillance for a time to discover travel patterns.

---

*Unpredictability is one of your best defenses.*

---

- Vary your mode of travel, i.e., car, taxi, subway, bus, walking.

- In airports, stay in VIP lounges or other areas behind security perimeters.

- Don't be conspicuous by dressing like a wealthy American (no three-piece "power suits") and don't travel in fancy cars or limousines and avoid parking in clearly labeled executive parking places.

- Don't carry impressive membership cards in your wallet; either leave them at home or in your suitcase. Carry pictures of children in your wallet (even if they're not your own!), as they may arouse lifesaving sympathy if you're abducted by a kidnapper or terrorist.

- If traveling by car try not to stop and, if possible, travel in caravan.

- When you can, avoid going out alone.

- Specially equipped cars can be purchased, or your car can be customized to maximize personal security.

- You can have your briefcase lined with a laminated ballistic armor. Similarly, you can buy a bulletproof clipboard. Both can serve as effective shields.

- Many different types of body armor are available, as well as such unique articles as "360° eyeglasses" which allow you to clearly see behind you.

- Don't put your business name or logo on your luggage ID tag or passport. **Don't advertise your executive status!**

- First-class airline passengers are prime targets during a hijacking. The first-class section usually becomes the command post, and by virtue of riding in first-class you will be considered a "worthy" hostage. Furthermore, first-class

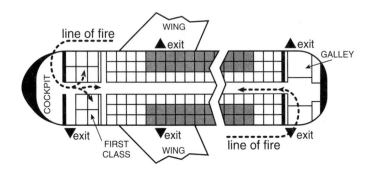

passengers are usually the last to be released by terrorists, and a rescue attempt will be directed at the cockpit and first-class section (hence the bullets may be flying).

- Sit towards the rear of the plane near an exit and not in an aisle seat; passengers sitting in aisle seats are most subject to terrorist abuse and may also be in the line of fire from a rescue effort from the rear entrance.

- When eating in restaurants or socializing in lounges, sit with your back to a wall to reduce your vulnerability, use any decorative wall mirrors to observe activity, and sit away from windows (not a good place to be in case of a bomb blast or shooting in the street).

- Register and leave your itinerary with the Consulate if you plan to stay in a foreign country for an extended business trip.

- If you believe that you are a high-risk target, consider taking a course in executive security and antiterrorist procedures from a reputable company.

**When approaching your car:**
- Have the car key in hand.

- Scan the area for suspicious persons and activity.

- Look in the backseat and on the floor for people or bombs that you did not leave there!

- Check the hood and trunk for any signs of tampering.

- Walk around the car and look for signs of tampering, e.g., new scratches, cracked windows or lights, or dust rubbed off (use a pocket flashlight if dark).

- Look for any markers such as fresh paint or reflective tape.

- Check to see if the car is as you left it, e.g., all doors locked and windows rolled up.

- Look under the car, around the tires and in the tailpipe for foreign objects.

- Examine the undercarriage for foreign objects or new or dangling wires.

- When you finally enter your car, do so quickly and lock the door behind you. Examine the dashboard for tampering and look underneath for objects or altered wiring.
- When driving, vary your usual times of travel and routes, drive alertly with doors locked and windows rolled up, and don't stop to help a "stranded" motorist.
- Keep your car in gear when stopped at a red light or stop sign, etc. Watch your rear view and wing mirrors.
- When driving in traffic, leave enough space between you and the car in front and to one side (especially at stop signs and lights), in case danger threatens and you need to turn out to effect an escape. See *Driving at Home and Abroad* on page 77 for additional precautions.

## Women Traveling Alone

- It is best to travel with at least one companion. Women traveling alone stand out and are obvious targets.
- For personal safety, dress and actions should not be provocative or seductive.
- You are less vulnerable if you travel light; a single piece of luggage is best.
- Don't hitchhike.
- Traveling alone in taxies should be avoided.
- Certain proprieties are considered necessary and appropriate for women in many areas. Proper clothing and observance of local customs may be important to your safety, e.g., in Middle Eastern countries women are expected to dress with exceptional discretion.
- With the exception of prostitutes, women in southern Europe do not go out alone at night, so have an escort.
- In some countries, such as Italy and Spain, be prepared to deal with the aggressive behavior of men.

- If walking or driving alone at night or in high crime areas, wear men's clothes, including a man's hat (put your hair up under it) and jacket to help disguise your sex.

- When returning late at night to your hotel alone, ask to be escorted to your room by a bellboy. If you are wearing any good jewelry, stop at the desk and have it put in the hotel safe. (See *How to Protect Your Money and Valuables*, page 52).

- See *How to Protect Your Person* on page 56, *If Followed* and *If Confronted* on page 90.

## Traveling with Children

When including children in your travel plans let them have some input. Be aware of what and how much they can handle and enjoy, and pace your trip for them.

- Children should always be accompanied by an adult or responsible person; never leave them alone to watch luggage or save a place in line, etc.

- Use the "buddy system" if there is more than one child.

- Their luggage should be packed separately in small bags so that they can manage most of their own.

- Keep children in sight or know where they are at all times.

- Establish firm ground rules regarding behavior.

- Children should always be accompanied to public restrooms, and take them with you when **you** go to the restroom instead of leaving them unattended.

---

> ***When traveling, carry a full-face photo
> of your child.***

---

- If one parent will be crossing international borders with his or her child, carry notarized permission from the other parent or else you may be denied entry into the country under suspicion of kidnapping.

- Use safety belts and other safety devices.

**Teach your children these safety behaviors:**
- Not to wander off alone.
- Always stay in sight.
- Never to go anywhere with a stranger.
- Never to run into the street.
- The name of the hotel/motel they're staying in.
- The names of their home town and nearest relative or friend.
- Respect for the police, school crossing guards, etc.
- What to do if lost.
- Children should be taught their parents first **and** last names.
- Always know where they are going if unattended and when they will return. Always accompany small children across streets.

## The Senior Traveler

Young muggers, purse-snatchers, con artists, and other assorted criminals see senior citizens as ideal targets, since they are not likely to give chase or fight back. For this reason, you should pay particular attention to *Mental Tactics for Staying Trouble-Free* on page 12, *How to Protect Your Money & Valuables* on page 52, *How to Protect Your Person* on page 56, *Women Traveling Alone* on page 42, *If Followed* and *If Confronted* on page 90, and the sections on public transportation, e.g., buses, subways, taxies.

Although all of the tips in **TRAVEL SAFELY** pertain to traveling senior citizens, here are some additional suggestions:

- Look for a travel agency or agent that specializes in working with senior citizens.
- Some travel agencies will deliver your tickets to your home, and some provide a shuttle service to the airport.
- Carefully and realistically evaluate the likely physical demands of the trip and your ability to meet them.
- Plan ahead for special dietary or medical needs (see *Health & Medical Preparation* on page 13).

- Plan ahead for special transportation needs. Your travel agent can help you make necessary arrangements, e.g., for a wheel chair at the airport if you cannot walk the distance to your departure gate.

- Don't be afraid to ask for help. If you ask for information, be sure you ask a reliable source, e.g. uniformed employees, police officers, tourist information personnel.

- Plan activities in small segments with periods of rest in between. Pace yourself; don't overdo it.

- Medicare **does not** assume responsibility for medical bills outside the United States. Insure yourself accordingly.

## The Handicapped Traveler

Carefully and realistically evaluate the likely physical demands of the trip and your ability to meet them. Pre-planning is a must. As long as you give advance notice of your requirements you are less likely to encounter serious problems. But do not take anything for granted. Check and double check! Be sure you understand everything clearly.

- Make a list of possible problems, e.g., water fountains, restrooms, theaters, crowds, on-site transportation, museums, the unkind person. The greatest barrier to travel by handicapped travelers is the fear of the unknown and the unexpected.

- **Carry an individual smoke hood in case of fire** (see *Appendix 1, Traveler Resources,* page 125).

- The statement, "Someone will always help" should be placed in the same category with, "The check is in the mail".

- Do not take anything for granted; travel brochures and sales information may exaggerate or be inaccurate.

- Many countries have not provided for easy access to places and services for the disabled.

- Although there have been some changes providing easy

access to sidewalks, stairways, and buildings, do not expect to find the structural environment easy going.

- Plan ahead, arrange for any special accommodations and transportation needs. Research your route and destination.

- Handicapped persons can expedite their clearance at customs by having all the necessary documents in order, e.g. visas and passports, lists of special medications, devices or other equipment needed.

- Each carrier establishes its own criteria which governs the transportation of handicapped/disabled persons. Each means of travel—airline, train, bus, car, public transportation, cruise lines or combinations thereof has its own challenges. These challenges may vary tremendously, especially with foreign domestic carriers. Call ahead.

- Travel during midweek when the number of passengers is usually less.

- Choose flights which involve the fewest changes of aircraft. Know your flight routes and how you are going to make connections. Check your times of arrival and departure so that you can make safe connections and are not left stranded somewhere in the middle of the night. Check out the availability of public transportation, rental cars and taxis which have special access equipment.

- Not too long ago, many airlines and other carriers required disabled passengers to have a current medical certificate, that they must be accompanied by a capable attendant, and set quotas (i.e., a maximum of 4 or 5 wheelchairs per flight). Generally, this is no longer the case, but check first for current rules.

- Expect pre-boarding and delayed de-planing since the handicapped are usually the first on and the last off. Therefore, arrive well in advance of your departure time.

---

*Many airlines require 24 hours notice*
*before departure time.*

---

- Deaf or hearing impaired travelers using hearing aids should request inspection by hand. If you are wearing a pacemaker for your heart, or if you are using an electronic guiding device for the blind, you should not walk through the metal detector and should request an inspection by hand.

- Because of the size and design of airplane lavatories, handicapped travelers should consider using the restrooms before departure. However, many new aircraft have designed more accessible lavatories on board. So ask when making your reservations.

- If you are physically handicapped or mobility impaired and you use metal or wooden canes or crutches for support, these must be relinquished once you are on board the aircraft. All will be returned to you before you leave the aircraft. If this poses a problem while you are on board discuss this with the flight attendants before boarding.

- Request a preflight briefing by flight attendants explaining emergency evacuation procedures, locations of oxygen masks, and other features of the aircraft necessary to ensure your safety. Practice a "mental rehearsal" of the safety

procedures. Mentally teaching yourself the necessary steps to evacuate the aircraft.

☛ Make sure you know where you are seated in relationship to the exits. It is helpful to brief those around you as to your special needs and skills which could help ensure everyone's quick and easy evacuation.

☛ You may have skills which will help others to find the exits and to remain calm. For example: if you are blind you have developed extraordinary skills in moving about and locating things without the use of sight. In a smoke-filled aircraft while wearing a smoke hood this would be invaluable. You also have learned to control panic reactions to unexpected situations.

- Dog guides used by blind passengers may travel in the aircraft at their masters feet, free of charge. Be sure to take care of your dog's needs before departure.

- Hearing impaired passengers should keep in mind that, in general, most hearing aids do not function well on board the aircraft. Be alert so that you do not miss any in-flight instructions or announcements which may endanger your safety.

- Learning disabled, mentally retarded and other developmentally disabled persons may require special attention for air travel. Passengers who cannot eat independently or care for their own personal hygiene on board the aircraft must be accompanied by a knowledgeable and trusted attendant.

- Evaluate your zones of vulnerability station by station, stop by stop. For example, the aircraft may stop at several cities and different people become your fellow travelers. Be alert to who gets on and off. Have contingency plans.

- You will usually be assigned a front seat on the aisle.

- Depending on the size of the plane, your wheelchair may or may not fit in the aisle, so you may have to use a boarding chair. Some newer models of aircraft have special design features for wheelchairs.

- Some airlines use a "handicapped lift", a portable enclosed elevator for use in airports without jetways.

- If your chair will be carried in the plane's baggage compartment, you may want to put it in a bicycle container (purchasable at the airport) for its protection.

- Make it clear to the airline that you will need your chair immediately on arrival at your destination.

- It is advisable to not travel with a battery operated chair because: (1) they are heavy and cumbersome and don't fold up; (2) they can be damaged in the baggage compartment; and (3) they will not be allowed on the plane if they use a spillable battery.

- If you are on oxygen, inform the airline beforehand; you may be subject to certain restrictions, e.g., your own oxygen supply will have to meet FAA specifications.

- Some airlines require that you have their staff physician's approval to use oxygen, so arrange for your doctor to speak with him.

- Flight attendants will tell you when the **seat belt** and **no smoking** signs are on and off.

- Some countries (e.g., Australia, Iceland, New Zealand) and Hawaii restrict importation of animals, including seeing-eye dogs.

- When traveling abroad with your guide dog, carry a *rabies inoculation certificate* and a current *health certificate* from your dog's veternarian.

- Hearing-impaired people should have their travel agent notify the carrier of their conditions and needs.

**When traveling by train**
- Inform the passenger agent of your condition and special needs.

- Plan ahead. Check out the details and contact a reliable source. Plan each step carefully from your front door to your destination and back. Call for reservations well in advance and be sure to explain your special requirements.

- Locations of accessible seating and restrooms by those

traveling by wheelchair are clearly marked on the outside of specific cars on some railroads. These cars carry the international access symbol on the outside.

---

*Amtrak has special accommodations for disabled passengers, but make reservations well in advance.*

---

- If possible travel with a trusted family member or companion. You increase your margin of safety substantially.
- Inquire in advance as to specific safety procedures to follow in case of derailment or any other emergencies.
- Check your times of arrival and departure so that you can make safe connections and are not stranded somewhere in the middle of the night. Check out the availability of public transportation, taxis, and rental cars which have special access equipment.
- Evaluate your zones of vulnerability station by station. For example, the train may stop at several cities and different people become your fellow travelers. Be alert to who gets on and off. Have contingency plans.

**When traveling by bus:**
- Most bus companies have programs which encourage mobility-impaired and other handicapped persons to travel by bus with a trusted and knowledgeable companion.
- Ask in advance about bus stations with user-friendly facilities, such as wheelchair lifts, accessible restrooms, lower phones, snackbar and restaurant open at convenient hours with automatic doors and special ramps.
- Plan your trip carefully from the moment you leave your home to when you return. Check your times of arrival and departure so that you can make safe connections and are not stranded somewhere in the middle of the night. Check out

the availability of public transportation, rental cars and taxis which have special access equipment.

- Ask what sections of town the bus stations are located. Is it a high crime area? If so, try to plan your trip by a different route.

- Evaluate your zones of vulnerability stop by stop. For example, the bus may stop at many different stations and different people become your traveling companions. Be alert to who gets on and off. Have contingency plans.

- If possible have your companion observe luggage transfers.

**When going on a cruise**
- Check with the cruise line first regarding necessary accommodations and equipment, and for any restrictions. Request a room on the lifeboat deck.

- Many cruise lines offer special accommodations for the handicapped traveler. Inquire before making reservations. Be sure to double check with a reliable source. It is difficult to change plans in the middle of the ocean.

- Evaluate your zones of vulnerability deck by deck while at sea and port by port when stopping over at a specific destination.

**Barrier free accommodations**
- Many hotels and motels, rental car companies, trains, and cruise lines offer specially equipped facilities for the handicapped. Make reservations as early as possible and **get confirmations in writing.**

- Most carriers will arrange motel accommodations for you, but double check yourself.

- There are many hotels, motels, and bed and breakfasts that have special accommodations for the handicapped person. They have rooms designed for easy access/egress and use. They have tried to remove architectural barriers in meeting rooms, restaurants and public restrooms. Facilities vary greatly throughout the world. Check with a reliable source.

- Plan ahead. Check with each of the accommodations as to their particular accessibility, since each chain or individual establishment has its own definition of user friendly and safe facilities.

- Do not rely on computer reservation information, call ahead and make sure that your special needs will be met. Do not take anything for granted!

- When making reservations ask such questions as: how wide is the bathroom doorway, are the grab bars strategically placed, whether restaurants and meeting rooms and public restrooms are accessible, does the room door have a dead bolt?

- **Carry an individual smoke hood in case of fire.** Ask about special procedures for the handicapped in case of fire or other emergencies. Additional locks may also be helpful.

- Ask the location of the place you plan to stay and its relationship to high crime areas. Many an unsuspecting traveler has wandered into an area where the locals fear to go.

**Check with local law enforcement.**

Read the other sections in this book carefully as the information applies to all travelers, handicapped or not. Consult *Appendix 1, Travelers Resources,* on page 125 for more sources of travel supplies and particular information.

## How to Protect Your Money & Valuables

Vacation spots are lucrative territory for professional criminals who recognize the tourist as easy and fair game. Many thieves, opportunists, and con artists "work" hotel lobbies and airline terminals where they watch potential victims for the "fatness" and location of their wallets. Your best defense is knowing that it can happen to you, so don't give the criminal the opportunity. **Don't make it easy for thieves!**

- First and foremost, don't be a victim of your own careless-ness, e.g., leaving your traveler's checks at the last hotel or on the writing table in the bank, misplacing your airline ticket, or leaving a restaurant without retrieving your credit card. **Research has shown that the main cause of losing your passport or having it stolen is** *carelessness!*

- Carry as little cash as possible as it can be easily lost or stolen and is not traceable; don't carry more cash than you can afford to lose.

- Carry only as much cash as you expect to need on any outing.

- Carry your checkbook only when you plan to use it. Other-wise keep it in a secure place.

- Don't keep your funds all in one place, i.e., keep part of your cash in a money belt and part in your wallet or purse, keep your traveler's checks separate, and even separate your credit cards. Separate your valuables as well, which minimizes the chances of losing all.

- Men should carry their wallets in zippered or buttoned pockets, or a front pant pocket.

---

***Never carry your wallet in your back pocket or "sucker pocket".***

---

- A thick rubber band wrapped around your wallet will secure its contents and make it less easy to "slip" out of your pocket.

- Women should always keep their purses on their person (never set it down unattended).

- Purses with strong shoulder straps are best; always put the strap over your head to discourage purse snatchers and, for maximum security, carry it under your sweater or coat. Purses should have a zippered inside compartment large enough to carry your money, traveler's checks, credit cards and driver's license, passport, and other important documents and valuables.

- For extra security, sew Velcro strips on pockets and purse flaps.
- Money belts, bra stashes, "shoulder-holster" and passport pouches, and leg and waist "safes" are good, but not foolproof measures. They can be ordered from a number of travel gear companies (see *Appendix 1, Traveler Resources,* page 125).
- Valuables are best kept out of sight. They can be kept in a pouch worn low around your neck, i.e., suspended from a strap or thong.
- Hidden pockets can be sewn into socks, bras, jackets.
- Never allow anyone to see into your wallet or purse to see how much you have; never display a large "wad" as it may invite trouble. Similarly, try to avoid exchanging money publicly as you may be watched while you stash your cash.

---

*To foil muggers, carry a second wallet: a "dummy" with expired plastic & little cash which you can surrender with a smile!*

---

- Be alert when using automatic bank teller machines.
- Choose an ATM in a building with 24 hour security, one that is in an enclosed kiosk preferably inside a building. Be sure to get a PIN number that can be used overseas.
- For small expenditures, e.g., taxi or bus fare, have smaller denominations and coins readily available in your pocket, so you don't expose your money or location of your wallet.
- Put some identification in your purse other than in your wallet; if your purse is stolen most thieves will only take your wallet and throw the purse away, so it may be returned if you have identification in it.
- If you have been foolish enough to have brought it, don't be ostentatious with your expensive jewelry. Wear it only in

places where it will not attract attention or in the case of rings, turn the stone toward your palm.

- Good watches with expansion bands are attractive to thieves since they can be pulled off easily.

- Keep your valuables in the hotel safe (get a receipt). Be watchful when you retrieve them as this is a time for a thief to try to distract you.

- To avoid becoming a victim of a "locker key switch scam", **don't let anybody help you,** when retrieving items storage.

- Thieves know to look in your camera bag for valuables.

- Divide your traveler's checks, cash, and credit cards between family members so you don't lose all if pickpocketed.

- Don't carry extra funds in your suitcase.

**Pickpockets have many favorite strategies:**
- Bumping into you.

- Playing drunk to get close, even hugging.

- Creating a disturbance, shoving or pushing in crowded areas.

- Keep your mind on your money, and your money in your shoes (figuratively **or** literally) if you're going out and about among the populace, especially at night in "colorful" areas of town.

- Immediately report any loss or theft to the police and request a copy of the report (get it before leaving the city, especially if abroad) to claim for insurance or a tax deduction.

- Take a minimum (preferably one) of credit cards, as "plastic money" is the first thing many thieves look for.

- Destroy the carbon in credit card charge forms if it still has one; crooks retrieve this **black gold** from trash bins and use the account numbers to order merchandise.

- Save all credit card receipts and compare them against your monthly statement to check for erroneous charges and merchants adding numerals to the actual charge amount. Notify your card company of any mistakes or discrepancies.

Half way across the country or around the planet is not the place to run short of money, so:

- Establish a budget and follow it. Set a daily spending limit.

- Stash some traveler's checks or cash in a tight front pocket for an emergency fund.

- Make arrangements with a family member or friend back home to cable you money if necessary.

- If you plan to stay in a particular city in a foreign country for a considerable time, consider opening an account at a U.S. bank that has an overseas affiliate for check cashing, wiring money, and other financial transactions.

## How to Protect Your Person

Personal safety means protecting yourself and family from harm and loss. The more you know about personal security, the better position you are in to remain safe. With proper knowledge, you can act and react appropriately, which reduces the likelihood of confrontation and physical harm. Furthermore, preparation brings with it some positive mental side effects that have a deterrent value.

The purpose of this section is to give you suggestions on how to prevent or avoid a possible confrontation, not on how to defend yourself if physically attacked, which is beyond the scope of this book (and cannot be effectively taught by a book anyway). If you want to learn how to physically defend yourself against a physical attack, seek training in self-defense from a qualified instructor.

- Crime data shows that the greatest potential of being mugged (i.e., robbed of your money or personal property) is between the hours of 5 and 10 p.m. on dark, lonely streets.

- Be observant when leaving a bank or using an ATM; be aware if anyone watches you come out and follows you.

- Walk against the flow of pedestrians to discourage anyone from following you. This also makes it easier to spot a pursuer.

- Always be wary of approaching strangers, cars, bicyclists and motorcyclists; all have been known to snatch purses and cameras.

*Statistically, you reduce your chances of being attacked by 70% if you walk with another person and 90% if with two others.*

- Walk in the center of the sidewalk away from parked cars as someone can throw open a door to knock you down or pull you inside.
- If walking towards a man who looks suspicious, take evasive action, or at least shift your purse to the side away from him.
- If followed by what you believe to be a mugger, drop your wallet or purse in a mailbox (be sure that he sees you do this). Then call the postmaster and arrange to have your property returned to you.
- Carry enough money in your wallet or purse to satisfy a mugger (say $20), and keep the rest in a tight front pocket.
- Before going out in a strange city, ask the hotel manager about "safe" and "unsafe" areas. Be sober when you go out among the populace; you're an easy target if tipsy.
- Wear little or no jewelry (even fake jewelry) in public places; thieves will literally grab and rip jewelry off their victims.
- Don't let strangers stop you on any pretext, e.g., for a light, to ask directions. Don't let strangers touch or crowd around you.
- If confronted you have the options of flight, fight, negotiation, doing nothing, or surprise and diversion (to effect an escape). Evaluate the situation quickly but rationally,

wiftly and with determination (see *If Con-*
ᵗe 90).

muggers recommend that you cooperate and
your money to avoid being hurt. If assaulted,
ver, they suggest running into the middle of the street.

---

*In the words of one mugger: "It's better to be a live*
*coward, than a dead hero."*

---

- Use everyday objects as weapons, e.g., keys between fingers, a fist full of coins, a pencil, bottle or glass.
- Women should carry a noisemaker, such as a police whistle or shriek alarm. Be careful of when you use a whistle, however, as you could get it punched down your throat.
- If in a foreign country, it's wise to learn a few words in the local language so you can call for help, e.g., police, fire, doctor (see *Appendix 2, International Vocabulary of Safety,* page 129).
- If you face a weapon, try to stay calm and assure your assailant that he has nothing to fear from you.
- If you fight back, it must be an **all out** effort!
- Carry names and numbers of persons to call in case of an emergency.

## Be Equipped: Know Your Weapons

Just as you should not venture away from home without a basic safety awareness, you should not be ill equipped. It is prudent to carry objects that might be used defensively, and to learn to recognize and use items in your environment defensively. However, the user must become proficient with any weapon. If you can't use it, it's useless or even dangerous. A weapon is nothing by itself; it is only as good as the person using it. With proper awareness, knowledge, and preparedness, you can be a veritable arsenal. Almost any object can be used to help defend yourself if you have the will to survive.

**Objects to take with you on your trip (depending somewhat on your destination) include:**

- A police whistle or shriek alarm.
- A walking stick, cane, or umbrella.
- A Swiss Army knife or equivalent.
- A belt-buckle knife.
- Mace, Taser, Pepper Spray (It is illegal to carry or pack pepper spray on board passenger planes, plan to purchase it at your destination).
- A metal handled flashlight.
- A money clip with a built in fingernail file for men, or a metal nail file with a solid handle for women.
- A miniaturized "hacksaw keychain" available at dime stores.
- See *Travel Safety Checklist* on page 32.

**Firearms are not recommended for the traveler** for several reasons: (1) they cannot be carried on airplanes or taken abroad; (2) they are illegal to carry concealed (even if you have a *concealed weapon's permit*, it is only valid in the issuing jurisdiction); (3) the risk of your weapon being taken away and used against you during a confrontation is considerable; (4) if used in a confrontation (e.g., to defend yourself against an assailant on the street), there is a chance of injuring an innocent bystander; (5) if it is lost or stolen it may be used in criminal activity against others; and (6) if you do use a firearm to defend yourself while traveling you may be in big trouble (the law will not necessarily be on your side), especially if you are unlicensed to carry it or did not have the legal right to use deadly force. (The same arguments generally apply to long knives.)

**Many ordinary objects in your hotel room can be used defensively:**

- Heavy objects (e.g., an ashtray) in a sock or pillow case makes a formidable club with which to strike an intruder.
- Lamps are dandy clubs.
- Boiling water, aerosol sprays, or rubbing alcohol from your

first-aid kit thrown in the eyes can be an effective deterrent against an assault.

- Pencils, pens, and keys make sharp jabbing weapons.
- Your electrical adapter (needed in many countries anyway) is a handy weapon when swung by its cord.
- A broken wall or dresser mirror provides a good cutting tool.

**Certain clothing and personal items can be used defensively:**

- Dental floss can be used for lowering or raising objects or notes, or to provide a trail to follow in the dark.
- Compact case mirrors can be used to expand vision into difficult places, to signal someone, or broken for their cutting edge.
- Shoe laces, nail clippers, needle and thread, and safety pins can have many uses.
- Razor blades make great knives.
- A shower cap can be used as a throwing sling (contrary to popular opinion, bras don't work well).
- A jump rope can not only keep you in shape, but the rope has multiple potential uses and the handles can be swung with great force.
- Scarfs and belts have multiple defensive uses.
- Luggage can be used defensively by thrusting it at an assailant, or as a shield against an attack (lightweight ballistic armor can even be sewn in one side).

## Natural Disasters

Every so often the unexpected and unthinkable happens: an earthquake, a fire, a flood or some other natural disaster. Routines must change drastically and contingency plans put in operation. These plans can be developed by using data gathered while doing the *Safety Scan Exercise* on page 63. If you are prepared you can reduce the fear, inconvenience and losses that accompany a disaster. (See *Travel Safety Checklist*, page 32.)

# Earthquakes

**Secure your home before you leave:**
- Secure shelves and top-heavy furniture, e.g., bookcases
- Move breakables and heavy objects to lower shelves.
- Secure overhead lights, heavy artwork, and mirrors.
- Strap water heater and gas appliances to the wall.
- Block the wheels/feet on large appliances, e.g. refrigerators
- Store flammable liquids outside.
- Equip gas appliances with flexible connectors.
- Secure valuables in burglar-proof fire resistant and crush proof containers in a safe place.
- Develop contingency plans

**During an earthquake:**
In commercial buildings such as office buildings, hotels and stores:
- Don't run for the exit, there may be a stampede. Stay on the same floor. Move away from windows.
- Stand in a doorway or crouch under some heavy furniture, e.g., a desk or counter.
- Do not use the elevator.
- Expect fire alarms and sprinkler systems to activate.
- Implement contingency plans.

Outdoors:
- Stay in the open, away from trees or other natural or man-made structures.
- Implement contingency plans.

In a vehicle:
- Pull to the side of the road as quickly as possible, but keep away from any natural or man-made structures.
- Remain in the vehicle until the shaking stops.
- Implement contingency plans.

**After an earthquake:**
- If trained to do so, treat the injured with first-aid. If not get help.
- Be alert and prepared for aftershocks.
- Put out small fires. Be careful around fires and possible gas leaks.
- Turn on your battery-powered radio for information and instructions.
- Watch for falling objects or structures about to fall down.
- Implement contingency plans.

## Floods

Floods are also a common and widespread natural disaster. Wherever you are, be aware of potential flooding hazards.

- Be aware of flood warning systems.
- Learn local evacuation routes.
- Implement contingency plans.

**In a vehicle**
- Watch for mud and rock slides.
- Do not drive through flood waters.

## Hurricanes

- Be aware of hurricane warning systems.
- Learn local evacuation routes.
- Implement contingency plans.

**In a vehicle**
- Drive only when necessary.
- Follow instruction of informed local authorities.

# The Safety Scan Exercise

This game is designed to help you develop your safety aware-ness and vigilance. Its purpose is to use the stuff of everyday life as a tool to enhance your travel safety and enjoyment.

The **first step** in the Safety Scan Exercise is to consciously ob-serve everything around you. Most of us blunder through the day in a state of half-sleep or lost in daydreams, oblivious to a large percentage of what goes on immediately around us. To the extent that you are in this condition you are vulnerable. To the extent that you are alert, observant, and aware, you are safer.

The **second step** in the Safety Scan Exercise is to put your in-creased safety awareness to work in protecting you by aiding in preventing jeopardy situations, and increasing your survival choices if in trouble.

The following exercises are designed to help you in this life-enhancing and life-protecting task.

**Exercise #1**

Observe your surroundings as if your life depended on it! Continually scan your environment to see how much you can see. If done sincerely you will be amazed at what you were missing.

**Exercise #2**

Note areas of safety that could be used during natural disasters, e.g., doorways, stairs, high ground, etc.

**Exercise #3**

Look for areas of vulnerability, e.g., recesses in buildings, alleyways, shrubbery, dark areas.

**Exercise #4**

When in public, try to spot suspicious persons and activity. Try to see everyone and size them up, e.g., who they are, what they do, their state of mind.

**Exercise #5**

Answer the questions: "How can I avoid these vulnerable areas and suspicious persons?" "What different routes can I take to vary my everyday routine?" Now do it!

**Exercise #6**

Examine your immediate area for escape routes and defensive positions.

**Exercise #7**

Answer the questions: What would I do if suddenly confronted? How would I respond, how could I escape, how could I defend myself?"

**Exercise #8**

Examine your person and immediate area for defensive objects. What are you carrying or what's around you that can be used as a self-defense weapon?

**Exercise #9**

Try to think and move as if you were a police officer or security guard, e.g., stay in defensible space, stay constantly alert for jeopardy, suspicious persons and activity. Look through his eyes.

**Exercise #10**

Look through the eyes of different types of criminals, e.g., pickpockets, muggers, burglars, rapists, and terrorists. Ask yourself, "How could they take advantage of me?"

# *On the Move*

## At the Airport

The airport has become a war zone. To help ensure your safety, observe the following precautions, but don't let paranoia spoil your trip; most airlines and airports do an excellent job in protecting you. In fact, the FAA now inspects foreign airports and carriers and the sky marshal program has been strengthened. Many airports have increased security beyond the usual baggage detection and screening systems by removing storage lockers altogether or placing them behind secured areas, doing away with curbside check-in on international flights, and allowing only ticketed passengers into the gate areas.

- On entering the airport take a few minutes and "size up" the situation. Practice your "natural warning system", i.e., let your intuition work for you. Be observant and stay alert.

- Observe the basic layout and floor plan of the airport and the location of all exits and emergency exits.

- Arrive early to avoid long check-in lines (this reduces your exposure in a vulnerable area).

- Move quickly to the appropriate counter to check your bags (**get a claim check for each one**), then proceed through the security check point where you are more secure.

- Move strategically, e.g., walk along walls to reduce exposure.

- Evaluate where you sit, stand, or wait in terms of defensive space, e.g., if waiting is necessary stay near an exit.

- Obtain your boarding pass before hand from your travel agent if possible to minimize your time in public areas.

- If you are flying on an airline that issues a computerized "confirmation number" in lieu of a ticket you must arrive early to choose a seat assignment and possibly stand in a long line at the departure gate. Be alert!

- Double-check your travel documents, e.g., passport, tickets, and departure information, i.e., date, time, flight and gate number.

- Try to stay away from telephone booths, unattended boxes, bags, packages, luggage, waste baskets, lockers or storage areas (they are nice places for terrorists' bombs).

---

*Don't accept a package from a stranger who asks you to transport it for him as a favor.*

---

- Avoid waiting near large glass windows in case of a bomb blast; if possible, wait near support columns and walls.
- Do not sleep while waiting for a plane. Be alert to what's happening around you.
- Use the airline club lounges or airport restaurants to avoid crowds at boarding gate waiting areas.
- If out of the country, mix in with the locals.
- Select a "safe seat" (see *Executive Safety* on page 39).
- After deplaning, claim your baggage immediately and leave the airport.

**Reducing the Risk of Terrorism:**
- ☛ Use the safest airports; try to avoid those that have a history of hijackings or terrorist incidents.
- ☛ Avoid traveling through airports in countries that are having political turmoil with ethnic or religious minorities.
- ☛ Avoid booking aircraft that originate or pass through trouble spots.
- ☛ Choose the safest airlines, e.g., don't fly Gaddafi Air!

- Airports are favorite places for pickpockets who have their eye on your vacation cash, so always secure your wallet or purse (see *How to Protect Your Money & Valuables* on page 52).
- Luggage thieves are on the loose in airports, so never leave your bags unattended at any time; either take them with you, have them watched by a companion, or lock them in a

storage compartment. Don't let yourself be distracted by strangers who might be setting you up, and don't nap.

## Trains

Trains are hotels on rails. There are many first class train systems around the world which are clean, fast, and on time. Others are extremely over-crowded with minimal accommo-dations and comforts, and never on time. Most of your train travel will probably be abroad.

- As always, travel light; redcaps and porters are often scarce, so you may have to carry everything yourself. Not only is this inconvenient, but you are more vulnerable to purse-snatchers and pickpockets.

- If you must take a lot of luggage, check it in the baggage car (if international border crossings or railroad regulations permit).

- For maximum security, book a private sleeper.

- To avoid waiting in lines and to make sure you have a seat or room, make reservations ahead of time for the popular trains. It also helps to travel on off days and hours.

- Be sure you understand military time or else you won't understand the train schedule.

- Try not to schedule a nighttime arrival as you may find yourself alone in an isolated area.

---

*Major terminals are mini-cities. They have all the amenities, conveniences, and security problems; they are frequented by pickpockets, robbers, and purse-snatchers in search of victims.*

---

- Unless you have a room reservation at a convenient hotel upon arrival, plan to arrive on an early train to give you plenty of daylight to find accommodations.

- Be sure you are at the right station; many cities have more than one railroad station.

- Make sure you are on the right train, in the right car, and that the car is actually going all the way to your destination (sometimes they're switched enroute!).

- Be sure you know how to pronounce and spell the city of your destination so that you'll recognize it when announced and can confirm it by looking at the city's name posted on the station, e.g., *Belgrade* is *Beograd* and *Florence* is *Firenze*.

- Immigration officials usually board the train at each border crossing, so have the necessary documents ready.

- If bothered by anyone or you observe suspicious behavior, notify the ticket booth personnel or conductor.

- Always keep your luggage near you and secure. Take it with you if you leave your seat, or cable lock it to your seat.

- Carry your own food or water (tap water on foreign trains is undrinkable), or be sure to have currency from each of the countries through which you'll be passing to purchase food and drink.

- Make an effort to know the service personnel so they recognize you; be courteous and patient.

- If you have a private compartment, learn your porter's name and ask him to give it when knocking.

- Be careful about getting off the train before reaching your final destination so that you don't get left behind.

## Buses

There are buses and then there are buses. Most private charter and tour buses are reputable and well organized. The most potentially hazardous type of bus travel is public bus transportation anywhere in the world.

- Bus terminals (like subway, train, and airport terminals) are areas frequented by robbers, purse-snatchers, and other criminals. Plan your trip so that you can avoid long waits in these areas, especially at night.

- When in a terminal, try to stay in view of uniformed employees. As always, stay alert; don't nap or read.
- There is safety in numbers so stand with others who are waiting.
- Keep physical control over your baggage, purse, and any other items. It may be prudent to use a security locker until departure if you have a long wait.
- If you need to use the restroom have a friend or companion watch over your luggage. If alone, use a security locker or take it with you.
- In many countries it is advisable to not travel alone on buses. Try to travel with a companion whenever possible.
- Select your seat carefully; scan the occupants before choosing a seat. Sitting in front close to the driver's observation is advisable.
- Sit in an aisle seat so that no one can trap you next to a window.
- Travel light so you aren't encumbered with excess baggage.
- Avoid arriving at night; you may find your destination is a dark, isolated, and deserted spot.

*Beware of persons who approach you
asking for directions or other
information. Keep a safe distance.*

- Carry some food and water on long trips.

- In many countries you can expect breakdowns and delays.

- When abroad, examine the bus if possible before you buy your ticket; if it looks in a state of disrepair, reconsider going.

- Wear comfortable clothes and walking shoes in case your bus breaks down in a remote area (which is likely in some countries).

- Avoid travel by bus in high-risk areas.

- Don't stand near the curb waiting for a bus as you're a target of criminals in passing vehicles looking for victims.

- Be aware of other passengers around you and report any unusual behavior to the driver. Stay alert.

- Don't sleep on public transportation; if you must, arrange your carry-on bags such that you will be awakened if anyone tampers with them.

- Hold firmly onto your purse, briefcase, or any carry-on bags. Don't put them on the seat next to you (an ideal opportunity for a grab-and-run artist). Carry-ons should be held in your lap or wedged between your feet.

## Subway

Subway systems are usually so large, complex, and deal with so many people (both good and bad) that they have their own police forces. But like police forces anywhere, they are understaffed and cannot be everywhere all the time, so observe these precautions:

- Avoid long, dimly lit, or vacant entrances to subway stations. Enter and exit at the end of the station where the clerk is on duty.

- There are usually more people and a conductor in the middle cars so choose your seat there. The last car is usually the most deserted.

- Avoid empty cars.

- When waiting for the next train, stand near the token booth. Don't stand near the platform edge as this is a favorite spot for pickpockets. There is also the danger of falling or being pushed onto the track.

- When waiting, be alert; don't get so involved in reading or daydreaming that you fail to notice a person approaching. Don't sleep.

- If waiting in a virtually empty station, have a shriek alarm or police whistle handy and a plan for quick egress.

- When on the subway, if you are bothered or threatened by anyone, try to find a conductor. Don't get off at your destination unless it's busy and well lit. If it's dark or empty, continue on to the first busy and well lit one, and then get off. If the person follows you, go directly to the token booth and ask the cashier to call the police.

- Beware of people jostling you on busy cars.

## Cruising

A cruise ship offers you a floating city with a hotel, restaurant, lounge, entertainment, and all necessary support services. In response to past terrorist activities, cruise lines are increasing their security measures, e.g., forbidding visitors aboard ship or requiring guest registration well in advance of sailing.

**To maximize your safety, pick a reputable cruise line and follow these tips once on board:**

- Study the deck plan and know the ship like you know your neighborhood back home.

- If you are subject to motion sickness, register with the ship's physician as soon as you board.

- Don't keep valuables in your cabin; leave them in the ship's safe or better yet don't bring any.

- Keep your cabin door locked at all times.

- Your cabin door lock may require the use of a key from the inside. If so, leave the key in the lock when in your room to avoid unauthorized entry and in case of power outage or nighttime emergency (so you won't have to search for your key and the keyhole).

- Look out for raised thresholds in doorways.

- Ship stairs are designed differently than ordinary stairs and decks may be damp from sea mist. Therefore, walk cautiously and use handrails. Wear rubber-soled shoes for extra traction.

- Do not attempt to get in or out of an upper berth without using the provided ladder as the ships movement may knock you off balance.

- Make an effort to get to know the ship's service personnel.

- Do not leave valuables laying near you or on your side table when lounging on the deck or anywhere on board (they are an easy and tempting target if you dose off).

- A cool breeze on deck masks the effects of the sun, so use plenty of sunscreen.

- Participate in the life boat drill and be familiar with the procedure.

- Know the ports of call and the procedures for going ashore. You are responsible for getting back to the ship **on time**.

- Attend all briefings on ports of call.

## Bicycling

Bicycling is a popular mode of travel around the world.

- Minimal safety equipment includes a front light, rear reflector, and reflective clothing or tape for night, a helmet with mirror, good brakes, guard clips for pants leg, and a cable lock (bicycle thievery is a major problem because of easy resale).

- Register and license your bicycle. The recovery rate for stolen bikes that are registered and licensed is as high as **ninety** percent.

- Insure your bike. It may be able to be included in the *household articles* floater of your home or renter's policy.

- Make frequent equipment checks. Move off the road to make any repairs.

- Know your route and carry good maps.

- Obey all traffic laws. Check at the police station for local laws pertaining to bicycling.

- If traveling in a group, ride single file.

- Watch for aggressive dogs.

- Eat and carry plenty of energy-rich food, drink plenty of fluids to prevent dehydration, and stretch frequently to avoid pulling muscles.

- Stay alert to approaching vehicles and pedestrians. Give them the right of way. Use hand signals to indicate turning and stopping.

- Do not carry passengers or ride between parked cars.

- Slow down, look, and listen at all intersections, alleys, and driveways.

- Travel in the same direction as the vehicle traffic; don't ride against the flow of traffic. Ride at a safe distance from all vehicles.

**The following antitheft precautions are suggested by the
Bicycle Institute of America, Inc.:**

- Never leave your bike unattended without locking it, even
  for a few minutes.  Lock your bike in a conspicuous place.

- Lock your bike to a stationary object with a heavy-duty
  case-hardened chain (or cable). Run the chain through the
  frame and both wheels, especially on quick-release hubs.

- Record your bike's serial number and take a color photograph of it. Carry these on your person, not on the bike
  when you travel to aid in police identification.

- As a further aid in identification, write your name and
  address on a piece of paper and put it under the hand grip
  or in the handle bar.

  **Many of the above suggestions apply equally to motorcycles.**

## Camping

If you plan to camp abroad, obtain an *International Camping
Carnet*, which entitles you to small reductions in fees.

- Take a minimal amount of quality functional gear and learn
  to use it well before you go.

- Pick your camping spot carefully, paying particular attention to its "feel", areas of vulnerability, its defensibility,
  protection from weather, and means of egress.

- If private property, ask permission first.

- If in a city, it's safest to stay in an established campground.

- Fires are illegal in most areas abroad, so carry a good stove.

- Put your valuables in the
  bottom of your sleeping bag
  at night (or in a sewn on
  inside pocket) and not in
  your backpack which is an
  easy target.

## Hitchhiking

Don't hitchhike unless you absolutely have to. If you must:

- Hitchhike with a companion if at all possible.
- When possible, accept rides only from women or older couples.
- Don't accept a ride from groups of men, speeders, or a driver who changes direction to pick you up.
- Before getting into the car, ask the driver for his destination before you indicate yours.
- Look in the back seat before getting in to make sure no one is hiding there.
- If there's more than one person in the car, try to sit next to a door; don't get sandwiched between strangers.

## In Your Recreational Vehicle

The popularity of recreational vehicles (R.V.s) in the U.S. is evidenced by the numbers seen on our highways. R.V.s are attractive targets for car burglars, since they are usually easy to break into and are filled with vacationer's property.

- Your R.V. is your home on wheels, so many of the security precautions that apply to your home apply to your R.V as well (see *Secure Your Home Before Leaving* on page 26).
- In addition, all the security precautions that apply to automobile travel apply to R.V. travel (see *Driving at Home or Abroad* on page 77).
- Stay in established campgrounds for maximum security.
- Don't let anyone into your R.V. that you don't know.
- Be extra careful of where you park if you must leave your R.V. unattended. Park in secure or highly visible areas to discourage car burglars. Check it often. Leave a light on or a portable radio playing and the curtains closed.
- When eating at restaurants, park out front and if possible, choose a table that gives you a clear view of your R.V. Similarly, when shopping, doing laundry, etc., keep an eye on your rig.

- Keep your R.V. in good operating condition.
- If you must carry valuables, construct a false drawer back or bottom, or conceal them in nondescript containers, e.g., under an empty food can in your cupboard. Car burglars have little time to search thoroughly.

## Taxies

Everyone who has traveled has a taxi story, be it humorous or serious. To keep from having your own story:

- Select your taxi carefully, i.e., don't ride in unlicensed "gypsy" cabs. Licensed cabs are required to post the driver's identification where it can be easily seen by passengers; make sure the photo matches the driver.
- Ask airport information or your hotel desk clerk to recommend a reputable taxi or limousine company.
- Learn the route to your destination (obtain a map or ask for directions), so you can determine that the driver is not taking you on an extra long route to run the meter up.
- Do not reveal personal information to the driver or to other passengers.
- If possible travel with a companion.
- If you feel uncomfortable or do not recognize the way, stop the taxi, get out, and catch another cab.
- Travel light. The more baggage you have the more you are burdened down, slowed down, and vulnerable.
- Don't get out in deserted or hostile looking areas.
- Thieves have been known to dash in and grab purses, cameras, etc., so don't sit right next to the door if you can't lock it. Keep your property secure (either clutched to your side toward the center of the seat, or held between your feet).

**If catching a taxi in a foreign country:**

- Ask at the airport or hotel for the approximate fare to your destination, then ask the driver. If it's out of line, take another cab.

- Negotiate the fare in advance with the driver if he doesn't have a meter. If there is a meter be sure that he uses it.

- Write down the address of your destination and carry it with you. Get the address written down in the local language in case the cabbie doesn't speak or read English.

## Driving at Home and Abroad

We are so accustomed to driving that we do not realize that it is one of our times of greatest risk.

- Know your destination and have a map.

- Plan your route carefully; estimate distances and time of travel. Allow plenty of time to get there.

- Be careful of "shortcuts" unless you really know the way.

- Time your road travel so you will be able to reach towns that will have gas stations open.

- Never let your gas tank get near empty. "Empty" should be defined as "half full".

- If traveling long distances or out in the country, pack what you might need should an emergency occur, e.g., a jacket, walking shoes, food and water, blanket, flashlight, flares.

- Wear seat belts and drive defensively.

- Monitor your car's "state of health". If you notice a problem, have it attended to as soon as possible before the car stalls on the road or you have a major problem.

---

*Don't leave your house key on your key chain when you leave your car keys with a parking attendant or mechanic, as it can be easily duplicated.*

---

- Plan to reach a comfortable and safe place before nightfall.

- Avoid local rush hours and dangerous areas of cities.

- Don't travel in congested areas with your windows open and doors unlocked as you become a target for all sorts of opportunists. Always drive with windows rolled up and doors locked.

- Keep your briefcase, baggage, and anything valuable in the trunk, even while driving.

- Keep all doors locked when the vehicle is parked and don't leave anything on the seats that may attract a thief.

- Avoid leaving your car unattended for long periods and try to park in safe places, e.g., busy or obvious locations.

- Avoid parking on side streets.

- At night, park only in well-lit areas (ones that will **still** be well-lit when you return to your car!) near your destination.

- Before getting out of your car, scan the immediate area for any loiterers and other suspicious persons (don't forget to use your mirrors to look behind you).

- Be especially careful in parking garages and dark or deserted parking lots.

- If parking in a private garage with an automatic door, watch your mirrors to be certain that no one enters behind you as the door is closing. If someone does, keep your doors locked and exit the garage.

- Avoid unsupervised parking garages.

- When approaching your car, if you see anything unusual such as people loitering near your car, keep a safe distance and wait for them to leave or seek help.

- Before entering a vehicle, check the front and back seats, especially at night, to make sure no one is hiding inside.

- If someone attempts to enter your vehicle with you in it, drive off. If you can't, honk your horn continuously.

- Be wary of detour signs or roadblocks (they may be there to set you up as a crime victim). If it doesn't seem legitimate, turn around.

- Don't allow yourself to be flagged down by anyone other than a policeman.
- Be suspicious of persons who may be disguised as public utility crews or road repair workers; lack of proper clothing or equipment may be evidence of phony work crews.
- If someone tries to pull you over by honking, don't stop; police don't honk, even unmarked/plainclothes units.
- If you need to drive through high-risk areas alone, seat an inflatable dummy (available from some novelty shops) beside you.
- Don't pick up hitchhikers.
- If lost at night, stop in a well-lighted conspicuous service station or 24-hour convenience store to ask directions.
- If you suspect that you're being followed by another motorist, don't stop or turn into a driveway, but continue to the nearest police or fire station, emergency room of a hospital, or stop at an open, well-lit and preferably busy service station to call the police. If none of these measures are possible, blow your horn, turn on your hazard lights, and blink your headlights. Try to get a license number and report it.

*Keep an old portable telephone under your seat. If you are followed by another car or harassed by pedestrians, haul it out and pretend to call the police.*

- If you often have to travel alone by car, buy a car phone.

- If you are harassed by another vehicle in an attempted bump-and-rob or carjacking situation on a multiple lane highway, drive on the inside lane which makes it difficult to be forced off the roadway, blow your horn, blink the lights and continue on to the nearest police station or busy, well-lit public service area. Try to get a license number and report it.

- If your car breaks down on the road, pull as far as you can off to the side, turn on your emergency flashers, raise the hood, attach a white handkerchief or article of clothing to the antenna, get inside, lock all doors and wait for help from a police officer. If a motorist stops, talk to him through a crack in the window and ask him to go for help.

- A handy aid for the stranded motorist is a large magnetic sign for help, e.g., CALL POLICE, that can be attached to the outside of the car. They are available from some travel gear companies (see *Appendix 1, Traveler Resources* on page 125). Sun block boards also have a similar message on one of the sides.

- To foil auto thieves, remove your distributor rotor or an ignition wire. Many sorts of hood locks, steering wheel locks, alarms, and other antitheft devices are available.

**If involved in an accident:**
- Summon the police and an ambulance, if necessary, as soon as possible.
- Stay until the police arrive.
- If there is any injury, administer first aid, but **do not** move anyone (in case of spinal injury).
- Take pictures if you can.

- Get names and addresses of witnesses.
- Exchange names, addresses, vehicle registration and driver's license numbers, and insurance company names and policy numbers.
- Don't admit fault or make any statement (other than for the police).
- Contact your insurance company.
- **Auto accident fraud** (when someone sets you up for an accident so they can make phony insurance claims) **can usually be avoided by following these tips:**
  - ☛ Drive defensively.
  - ☛ Don't tailgate.
  - ☛ Observe the cars around you and be alert for a set-up. Accident stagers often use older, beat-up large cars which pull in front of you, then stop suddenly to avoid the "swoop" car that changes lanes suddenly in front of them.
  - ☛ Be especially cautious if you are alone, drive a fancy car, or are well-dressed (stagers will think you're well insured).
  - ☛ Stagers like to target commercial vehicles since they are usually heavily insured.

---

*Hanging clothes in the backseat of your vehicle identifies you as a tourist or business person, so don't.*

---

### Car rentals

If you plan to purchase, lease, or rent a car in a foreign country, check for details with your travel agent and automobile association; advance planning can save you a lot of aggravation and money. Driving in a foreign country can be

a foreign experience. Follow these additional guidelines to prevent becoming a target on the road:

- An *International Driver's License* may be necessary if you want to drive a vehicle. It is available at most **A**merican **A**utomobile **A**ssociation offices.

- An *Inter-American Driving Permit* is available in the western hemisphere.

- The less known *Carnet* is an international customs document for automobiles and, in effect, a passport for the vehicle.

- Some Western European countries accept a valid U.S. driver's license, but be sure it won't expire during your trip.

- Check your automobile insurance for coverage abroad.

**When renting a car overseas:**

- Avoid models that identify you as an American or as someone fairly rich or important.

- Check the company's "drop-off" policy for restrictions or extra charges.

- Before selecting a rental company, ask if there are offices in the areas you will be traveling.

- If insurance comes with the car, or you purchase additional insurance, ask just what it covers.

- Ask the rental agent about driving laws and customs, road signs, and maps.

- Before hitting the road, familiarize yourself with the car and all its controls; if necessary, ask the agent.

- Learn to recognize the universal traffic signs (see *Appendix 3, Universal Signs*, page 130).

- Familiarize yourself with metric speed and mileage. To convert metric, divide the figure by 10, then multiply by 6, e.g., 100 kph ÷ 10 = 10 x 6 = 60 mph. (see *Appendix 4, Metric Conversion Table*, page 132).

- Travelers in foreign countries are much more prone to accidents, and safety measures (e.g., guardrails and seat belts) are minimal if not nonexistent.

- Driving or being driven in another country can be hazardous. Driving skills and customs vary greatly and you can encounter wild traffic in the cities, unmarked, rough, narrow, steep, or winding roads in the country, and roads crowded with animals and people.

- In some countries you will have to adapt to the steering wheel on the right and driving on the left side of the road.

---

*When stopped at restaurants, don't examine your map as this identifies you as a traveler unfamiliar with the country.*

---

- Inform someone (family member, friend, companion) of your route, destination, estimated time of arrival (ETA), and date of return.

- If traveling off the beaten track, during unusual hours, or in strange country, check beforehand with the car rental agency or hotel clerk for locations of service stations on your route.

- If you find a group of kids hovering around your car as soon as you park, either find another location or pay the group leader a pittance to watch (and protect) your car. If you don't, you may find that some damage has been done when you return.

- Expect legal trouble if involved in an accident.

## Crossing Borders

Customs bureaus are one of the oldest institutions in any country. All custom agents are trained to foil attempts to bring objects into their country illegally. You don't have the one untried method!

- Customs services prohibit and restrict many articles (e.g., some countries restrict importation of gold and jewelry). Check with the Customs service beforehand to be sure; don't rely on second-hand information.

- Be courteous and quiet when going through Customs.

- Answer all questions directly. Don't volunteer any information or you may appear suspicious.
- When asked what your travel purpose is, reply, "Pleasure". It is recommended that you should not volunteer any professional information that might identify you as a target.
- Have all travel documents available, e.g., passport.
- Dress and act conservative and be well-groomed.
- Keep all merchandise receipts and have them handy.
- Don't get paranoid or jump to any conclusions; all officialdom has its rituals, red tape, and unexplainable delays and procedures.
- If driving another person's car, you will need written permission from the owner to cross borders.
- Similarly, you will need written permission from the parents of a minor you're taking over a border.

# The Traveler

## Foreign Cultures & Traditions

When in a foreign country you can enhance your personal safety by not violating local traditions. Dress, behavioral expectations, and standards of right and wrong vary greatly from country to country.

**Remember: you are a guest in a foreign country.**

- Familiarize yourself with the customs of the country you will visit.

- Try not to violate unwritten dress codes. Your clothing can sometimes offend people, e.g., short shorts, certain colors.

- Eating and drinking customs vary greatly. The manner in how you eat and drink is as diverse as what you eat and drink. Dinner can be as early as 4 p.m. and as late as midnight.

- The language barrier can be frustrating, but remember that the people in other countries may not speak your language for the same reasons that you do not speak theirs!

- Be sensitive to names. Many countries list the last name first, while others combine the father's and mother's name. For example, in China the surname is given first, but in Taiwan the Christian name is often first. In Spanish-speaking countries the father's name is first, but in some Portuguese-speaking countries the mother's name comes first. Be sure to ask.

- Simple courtesies and good manners are recognized every-where, although what constitutes good manners varies greatly. **It is usually NOT a good idea to:**
  - ☛ Use first names unless asked to.
  - ☛ Conduct business at times other than customary.
  - ☛ Photograph anyone without permission.

**It is usually a GOOD idea to:**

- ☛ Use proper names and titles.
- ☛ Be genuine and smile!
- ☛ Keep proper distance.
- ☛ Avoid long periods of eye contact.

- Acquaint yourself with major nonverbal signals as this may keep you out of trouble, e.g., a head nod signals "yes" in most countries, but in others it can mean just the opposite, and various common gestures in this country may be obscene in others.

- Learn the local sentiments towards touching. Hugging is as common as the handshake in Latin and Slavic countries, while the Japanese avoid casual physical contact. Shaking hands is not a universal greeting.

- ☛ Observe local holidays.
- ☛ Be alert to local biases and prejudices.
- ☛ Don't be loud, condescending, or a conspicuous spender.
- ☛ It is usually wise to avoid discussing politics, religion, and sex.

**Make an effort to "blend in":**

- *Wearing proper clothing:* conservative clothing that you look and feel natural in and fits in with your surroundings. Avoid wearing loud, gaudy, unusual clothing and flashy jewelry, even if fake.

- *Proper behavior:* inappropriate behavior makes you stand out as much as clothing. Attempt to observe and follow local behavioral customs. Don't gawk unnecessarily like a tourist, or drape several expensive cameras around your neck. If you smoke, switch to local brands (foreign brands identify you as a visitor).

- *Proper attitude:* blending in is as much a state of mind as it is appearance. Show respect for local customs, beliefs, and laws. Don't exclaim: "Oh look, Darling, aren't the natives cute!" or "Isn't that custom silly!" Try to bridge the intercultural gap by reading up on your destination before arriving.

## Safe Sight-seeing

### Sensible Sight-seeing

When walking in public areas, as an executive or tourist you must be vigilant. Learn to recognize potentially dangerous situations and to take the necessary precautionary steps to reduce or avoid them. Continually ask yourself: "How do I recognize and avoid dangerous situations?" You can learn to avoid being an easy victim and how to protect yourself (see *The Safety Scan Exercise* on page 63).

- Don't broadcast your sight-seeing plans in public; you could be followed or return to find your room burglarized.

- Plan your route ahead of time to avoid fumbling with a map on an unfamiliar street. This identifies you as a stranger in a strange land.

- For maximum security, hire a private guide.

- Assess your physical ability; determine how far you can walk, and know your destination.

- The way you walk can attract or discourage attention; be natural but confident, stand tall and walk briskly.

- Through proper body language and a positive attitude of self-respect, you will be seen by predatory criminals as not easily intimidated and a high-risk target.

- Maintain a low profile by not looking like a "tourista." The more you stand out as a stranger, the more your risks increase.

- Be alert and observant. Anticipate potential danger.

- Carry your purse with the strap over your head and

in close to your body like a football. Carry it so the opening flap is towards you.

- Carry your wallet in a secure pocket; usually a front pants pocket is best, or an inside blazer button-down or zippered pocket (in the absence of a button a safety pin can save you your money!).
- Avoid having to wait or stand in one place for too long as this brings attention to yourself.
- Know your route and avoid shortcuts, especially through parks and alleys at night. Mentally map out your route and look for landmarks.

-----

***Don't allow anyone to stop you or crowd around you, keep moving.***

-----

- Keep your hands free.
- Be aware of and visually check out blind spots and "places of opportunity," e.g., recessed doorways, alleys, shrubbery.
- Note defensible spaces and places of safety, e.g., well-lighted areas, places with a lot of people, public buildings, churches, hotels.
- Always be alert for suspicious individuals and potentially dangerous situations.
- In large cities at home or abroad, watch for street gangs. Take precautionary evasive action if necessary.
- When walking after dark stay close to the curb, away from dark alleys and doorways. If the street and sidewalks are empty, walk down the middle of the street.
- If you need to go out alone at night, let someone know where you're going and when you expect to return.
- During the daytime, walk down the middle of the sidewalk to negate the possibility of falling victim to a grab-and-run motorist, bicyclist, or motorcyclist.
- If not incongruous, carry a walking stick, cane, or umbrella.

- Pay attention to your intuition and, more importantly, act on it, i.e., if you sense danger in front or behind you, take evasive action and seek a safe place until it passes.
- When you stop to sight-see, assess what's happening around you from a safety standpoint; combine sight-seeing with reconnaissance.

*Just as you drive defensively, sight-see defensively!*

- Act as if you know where you are going, even if you are lost.
- Be cautious of strangers who stop you to engage you in conversation. Maintain a critical distance, your first line of defense.
- It's safest not to respond to requests from cars that pull over, just keep on walking.
- Be alert for a car occupied by young men parked at a crosswalk with the motor running; avoid it by changing routes.
- Be alert for and avoid crowds of youths. Take evasive action if necessary. In Europe, avoid groups of Gypsy children who crowd around you; they are professional pickpockets.
- Travel light when walking or else you will prematurely wear yourself out and make yourself a more desirable target for muggers.

*If you choose to respond to a driver who stops to ask you directions, stay a safe distance from the car.*

- If bothered by a driver in a car, walk in the opposite direction or cross the street.
- If you ask directions of a stranger on the street and he or she offers to take you to your destination, be suspicious.

- If in trouble, seek sanctuary in a private business or public building, e.g., police station, post office, fire station, hospital.
- If you can, always walk with a companion or group.
- Avoid crowds and civil disturbances of any kind, and don't get involved in disputes with locals. Stay away from areas in which you have no business.
- Children and beggars in some foreign countries are taught to setup tourists for pickpockets, so don't let them (or other strangers) stop you; keep on walking and shake your head "no".
- If you are being followed in a lonely area, run to the nearest house in which lights are on and ring the bell, pound on the door, or shout "fire!", not "help". (See *Appendix 2, International Vocabulary of Safety*, page 129).
- Don't hesitate to attract attention. If the situation is urgent, break the nearest window or pull a fire alarm if handy (often they are located on street corners).
- See *How to Protect Your Person* on page 56.

## If Followed

First, determine if you are actually being followed by varying your pace or changing direction. If you are convinced that you are being followed:

- Cross the street.
- Try to lose yourself in a crowd.
- Make your way to a police station.
- Go to a phone and call the police.
- Pretend to see a friend and call out and wave.
- If at night, stay in well lighted areas.
- See *How to Protect Your Person* page 56 for additional suggestions.

## If Confronted

You've done everything you could think of to avoid trouble, yet you are confronted. Your out-of-town status tells a criminal that you are not likely to press charges, and that you may be carrying extra cash. Realize that he is nervous, in a hurry, and probably just wants your money and valuables.

- Self-protection is **not** based solely on physical size and athletic ability. Mental preparedness is an equally important factor.

- Your first response in any jeopardy situation is crucial. Control your first response. Act decisively, quickly, and with confidence.

- The element of surprise is your assailant's first weapon, so rob him of this by being alert.

- Ask yourself some basic questions: How can I get out of this predicament? How serious is it and what's my risk of bodily harm? Can I escape or simply walk away? What are my alternatives? What objects are handy that I can use as weapons? Is there help nearby and what's the best way to summon it, e.g., yell "fire!"?

---

*Your primary goal is to survive unharmed, so give up your property. Don't foolishly fight to retain it.*

---

- Run away if possible.
- Try to stay calm and get a physical description of your assailant to relay to the police.
- Get away as quickly as possible and report to the police.
- If the attack is physical and you stand the chance of harm, a spirited show of resistance will often be an adequate defense, including shouting or screaming, hitting, biting,

kicking, eye gouging, etc. Anything less than an all-out effort and commitment is unacceptable. Pleading for mercy with your assailant is usually a mistake. Know when to give in and cooperate in order to stay alive.

- See *How to Protect Your Person* on page 56 for additional tips.

## Safe Shopping

Shopping is one of the benefits and favorite pastimes of traveling to foreign countries. To do so safely, observe the following precautions:

- Carry enough currency in small denominations.

- Learn the denominations and to count the local currency so you are not at the mercy of clerks. Learn the metric system (See *Appendix 4, Metric Conversion Table*, page 132).

- Be discreet with your "wad". Women should peel off the necessary bills inside their purse without removing their wallet. Men should open their wallets towards them so the contents can't be seen.

- Avoid carrying packages in your arms; a cloth or fishnet sack or day pack is advisable. If you do have your arms full of bags, don't let your purse dangle off your elbow. If grocery shopping, have a box boy carry your bags to your car.

- Before buying an object, ask yourself if it will travel well.

- Beware of "tourist traps" that sell inferior goods at high prices.

- If you buy food on the open market select it carefully and wash or preferably peel all vegetables and fruits. Avoid meats unless you have refrigeration and don't drink milk (many countries do not have the strict quality control and health standards that the U.S. has).

- In most countries it's wise to avoid street vendor foods.

- Be alert to counterfeit labeling on cans, packages, and bottles.

- While shopping you are particularly subject to con artists, opportunists, and thieves who frequent the same areas.

- If anyone approaches you or strikes up a conversation be alert for a possible setup.
- If you buy jewelry or precious stones, be cautious of fraud. It is advisable to deal only with reputable merchants or have the stones appraised by a certified gemologist first.
- If you need to ship purchases home, it's safest to do it yourself. This prevents the problems of *misaddressed* packages, *nonreceipt* of packages, and receipt of *wrong* packages.
- Keep the bill of sale. It should specify shipping date, estimated date of arrival, an itemized list of contents, and the insured value.
- If you have packages shipped home, always insure them.
- If you have packages freighted home, get a bill of lading.
- A *Value Added Tax* is levied on items purchased in many European countries. If you ship the items home you may be able to avoid the tax. If not, ask the store clerk for a refund application.
- Keep all sales receipts as you may need them at Customs.

**To bargain effectively:**

In many countries you are expected to vigorously bargain; if you don't you will pay very inflated prices. Bargaining is often customary in open markets and bazaars, but not in big-name shops. Before shopping, ask what the local practice is.

- Dress down.
- Be indifferent and restrained; don't telegraph your strong like for an item or your desire to have it.
- Decide in your own mind what an item is worth and what you're willing to pay for it.
- Make a reasonable offer, generally half of the asked price.

- Then inch your way upward in a series of offers and counter offers, but go no higher than the price you've set in your mind.

## Photographing

- There is a direct relationship between the number and size of your camera equipment and your vulnerability and safety. It is wisest to use a small pocket camera that can be carried in your jacket or purse.

- Always keep your equipment attached to your person or under immediate surveillance and control; tourists who set their equipment down even momentarily have had it snatched up by grab-and-run opportunists.

- Inform yourself of local restrictions on the use of cameras, e.g., photographing religious objects, services and ceremonies, (in many countries they are considered holy and not to be photographed without permission), police and military personnel and installations, border areas, industrial structures including harbor, rail and airport facilities, some historical sites, civil disturbances, and some people object to being photographed.

- If you'll be taking very expensive camera equipment, have the original purchase invoice or sales slip as it may save you trouble at Customs checkpoints.

- Carry exposed film on you or in your carry-on bag. If in your carry-on bag request that it be hand-searched at airports (some electronic detection devices can damage exposed film).

- Carry your camera on the plane; if packed in your checked luggage it could end up lost or damaged.

*To protect your exposed film from the damaging effects of radiation, buy a lead-lined pouch (see Appendix 1, Traveler Resources, page 125).*

- If you deplane during a stopover, take your camera with you; don't leave it in the overhead storage compartment. You may even take it and other valuables to the lavatory if traveling alone.
- Carry your camera in a plain bag that won't lure thieves.
- Always keep your camera bag zipped up to help foil thieves.
- If touring by car, don't leave your camera in the trunk or glove box as it will be vulnerable to theft and damage by extreme heat.

## Eat, Drink and Make Merry Safely

Eating, drinking, and making merry are some of the attractions of foreign travel.

- Select your restaurants and night clubs as carefully as you select your lodging and transportation.
- Don't flaunt your American identity when abroad and stay away from restaurants and bars frequented by U.S. servicemen, who have been terrorist targets.
- Note the location of exits and fire escapes in all restaurants, lounges and bars, etc.
- It's a good idea to drink only bottled beverages in any country or area where the water is likely to be contaminated. Request that the bottle be opened at your table in your presence.
- Ordering blind from foreign menus may offend the sensibilities of your palate and be hazardous to your digestion, so, unless you are very daring, buy a *menu translation guide*.
- When in Rome do as the Romans do. Observe local

customers to get clues as to appropriate behavior and local traditions.

- Examine your bill carefully as sometimes it may be difficult to read, e.g., Europeans write their 7's differently.

- When a guest in a foreign home, a "thanks but no thanks" may be tantamount to rejection of host and country.

- Similarly, toasting (often to excess) is equivalent to our handshake and a refusal to participate is equal to a rebuff.

- Be courteous, quiet, and don't stay too late.

- When a guest in a foreign home, do as your host or hostess does, e.g., if they go shoeless, do likewise.

- Watch with whom and where you make merry; sexually transmitted diseases are on the increase.

- Be cautious with any new acquaintance as he/she may be an opportunist.

**Tipping**

Tipping practices vary greatly from country to country. Tipping in the States is customary, but in countries like Japan and Thailand it isn't customary at all. Overtipping and undertipping are universally offensive. To avoid offending service providers, paying too much, and putting yourself at risk or being embarrassed, observe these guidelines:

- Find out what the tipping policies and customs are from your travel agent, tour guide, desk clerk, etc.

- In restaurants, check to see if a service charge has already been added to your bill, a common practice in many countries. If you do not see a notice on the menu or marked on the check, ask the waiter or maitre d' if it's included. Even if a service charge is included, tip the maitre d' if he performs some extra service, e.g., given you a special table, or prepared dishes at tableside.

*In some countries tipping is even an insult, e.g.,
China, Iceland, and Tahiti.*

- A rule of thumb is to tip 15-20% of the bill in restaurants.
- Most tour packages include all tips for services, but ask before signing a contract.
- Generally, you should tip your cabbie (unless a service charge is included on the meter as in Belgium, Denmark, and the Netherlands), maitre d', waiter, wine steward, baggage porter, doorman, bartender and chambermaid, concierge, washroom attendant, theater usher, and anyone else who provides you any additional or extraordinary service.
- Cruise lines sometimes include tips in your ticket price. Ask before you go. If they aren't, ask about proper and expected tipping practices once on board.
- Airline personnel are not tipped.
- Hotel maid service is usually included in the price of the room, so tipping is unnecessary unless you ask for special favors and services. Tip room service. Tip the concierge (hall porter) if you request special favors or services. If you plan to stay a long time, tipping will grease the wheels of service and help your stay be more pleasant.

**Foreign Currencies**

Unless you pre-plan and familiarize yourself with foreign currencies and conversion rates and procedures, you will be playing a game of currency roulette.

- To get the most favorable rate, exchange money at reputable banks or traveler's check offices (preferably the same company that issued your traveler's checks)
- Avoid exchanging money stateside, in airports, train stations, hotels, or with money changers. This is especially important in areas of political instability because the currency changes frequently. You may be given old bills which are no longer legal currency.

- Many places will give you a better rate of exchange for actual greenbacks rather than traveler's checks since they require less processing.
- Often the best exchange rate is in the country visited, so exchange only a little U.S. currency before entering the country.
- Street money changers may offer higher exchange rates than the official one. Some governments ignore this practice while others may arrest you, so don't take the chance.
- You will save transaction fees if you exchange large amounts instead of frequent smaller amounts, but it's safest to lessen the impact of theft or loss by buying traveler's checks in small denominations (e.g., $40 or less) and cashing them one at a time.
- It is cheaper to cash checks if they are in the local currency. Therefore, you will save fees if you buy traveler's checks in the currencies of the countries you plan to visit. Ask your traveler check company if they offer checks in foreign currencies.
- If you carry coins across a border you may discover that you can't exchange them, therefore convert them to paper before leaving the country.

---

*Don't freak out when your waiter presents you with a check for 32,000 lire (about $20)!*

---

- To prevent being taken advantage of by opportunistic merchants and waiters, be sure you understand the country's money denominations so you can calculate and pay your own bills.
- Learn the relative value to the dollar of the local currencies so you can estimate the value of goods and services.
- Some countries require that you exchange a minimum amount.
- Other countries have regulations on how much (if any) of

the local currency you can bring into the country and even how much you must spend each day. Unless you can show proof that you reached the spending limit when you leave the country, you may be unable to exchange the local currency for dollars.

- **Tip packs** with coins and small bills can be purchased at many U.S. international airports. They are handy when you first arrive in a foreign country for small expenses, e.g., taxi, phone, tipping.

## Conducting Business

Knowing the protocol, customs, and etiquette of a foreign country in which you plan to do business may be crucial to your success. **Know the rules wherever you are**.

- The ultimate passport abroad is your business card.

- Business dress should be very conservative, i.e., dark suits for men and dresses or suits for women.

- Schedule your business trip so that you avoid holy days; would you want a foreign businessman to visit you over Christmas?

- Know when it is appropriate to conduct business, e.g., in some countries it is verbotem to talk business after business hours, whereas in other countries there is no such restriction.

- Always be on your best conservative behavior, e.g., in Europe never use first names without being asked, always be buttoned up and avoid the distinctly American informalities of taking your suit coat off and loosening your tie, talking with hands in your pockets, chewing gum, backslapping, and propping your feet up on the desk. Also, use appropriate titles and academic degrees to show respect, use a soft handshake, and be punctual.

*Research and observe proper protocol, e.g., in Germany gentlemen walk and sit to the left of men of senior business rank and of all ladies.*

- Research local nonverbal communication signals as they may be crucial to the success or failure of your business purpose, e.g., in Bulgaria a nod of the head means "no" while a shake means "yes," and the "thumbs up" gesture is considered rude in Australia.

- Gift giving is expected on first business encounters in some countries, in others it is expected only after the first meeting, and illegal in others. Gifts too modest are as bad as gifts too expensive or extravagant. Find out before you travel.

- See *Foreign Cultures & Traditions* on page 85.

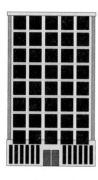

## In Your Motel/Hotel

It is your responsibility, or that of your travel agent's, to find lodging that meets your standards. Accommodations vary greatly, ranging from luxury hotels to boot camps. Many travelers have war stories to tell about their lodgings. To avoid having your own war stories, observe the following precautions and recommendations:

- Stay only at reputable motels and hotels.

- If traveling by auto, choose motel/hotels with secure on-premises parking.

- For motel/hotel guests the most vulnerable places are the parking lots, indoor garages, corridors, and elevator. Don't linger or wander unnecessarily in these areas and be alert for suspicious persons or behavior.

- Reservations assure a place to stay and save time, but you are renting sight unseen.

- Call the hotel before you arrive, not just to confirm your reservation but to ask for the best route from the airport. At this time advise them as to your estimated time of arrival to the hotel.

- Upon arrival at your hotel by taxi, airport bus, or limousine, stay with your luggage until it's brought into the lobby (don't dash in to register and expect your luggage to magically follow). Similarly, make sure your luggage is placed in the taxi, airport bus, or limousine after checking out.

- When registering, sign your last name and first initial only, and don't use titles or degrees. This makes it more difficult for anyone to determine gender, marital, and professional status.

- If driving and you park in a garage or parking lot, you may be asked to leave the ignition key in the car or with the attendant; if so, remove your trunk and house key.

- Muggers, pickpockets, and assorted con artists like to work hotel districts. Thieves even con their way onto hotel/motel staffs.

- The location of the hotel, motel, hostel, or inn is an important component of security, e.g., is it in a good area of town?

- An important security consideration when choosing a room is the exterior windows. Ground floor windows are easily reached and accessible to burglars and other criminals, as are windows near fire escapes and adjacent roof lines. Depending on the immediate environment around the facility, the quality of neighborhood and level of security protection, it may be advisable to request a room on the second floor or above and not immediately adjacent to a fire escape or other means of access. This must be weighed, however, against the fire danger, existence of a sprinkler system, number of and access to fire escapes, etc. (see *Motel/ Hotel Fire* on page 106).

- Inspect your room to be certain that the door locks work, that the windows can be secured, any door to an adjacent room is locked from your side, and that the phone works. If not, ask for another room.

*When absent from your room make sure it seems occupied. Leave a light on, the TV or radio playing, and vary the pattern.*

- Ask the maid to make up your room while you're at breakfast, then when you go out for the day put the **Do Not Disturb** sign on the door.

- Always lock your room door when absent and keep your room key with you, even if gone for only a few minutes.
- Lock any windows and sliding glass doors.
- Instruct the desk clerk not to give out your name or room number. Ask the clerk to call your room if someone inquires.

- If the hotel parking attendant puts a parking sticker on your windshield, be sure your room number isn't on it (always keep your room number private).

- Don't try to outsmart thieves by hiding valuables in your room.

- Take along a portable door-locking device, such as a **travel lock** or **wedge**, as it can be used at night or when in the shower to prevent entry by unauthorized key holders. Keep the key in the lock so you can exit quickly in case of emergency (make sure your security is not a trap!)

- A travel lock can be used during the day to lock up your valuables and clothing in the closet (if your room has one) or a drawer, however, it's best to use the hotel safe.

- If you must leave valuables in your room, buy a "safe hanger". It looks like a large clothes hanger, but contains a locked compartment large enough for valuables (when covered by a coat or dress it resembles an ordinary hanger).

- When in the room, keep your key in the locked door.

- A standard wire hanger can be used to prevent your door lock from being picked or the key turned or pushed out from the outside. Run the hanger loop through the hole in the key end, then the door handle.

- Carry some envelopes in which you can seal your valuables and leave with the clerk to put in the hotel safe. Get a receipt. Hotel envelopes are too universal.

- Create your own "intrusion detection system" by moving furniture in direct and usual passage routes in your room so that an intruder will have a difficult time surprising you in the dark.

- If the door locks are insufficient and you don't have a travel lock or wedge, prop a chair under the door knob or request a different room.

---

***Don't leave valuables in your room as there could be unauthorized copies of your room key floating around.***

---

- For extra security, buy a portable cordless electronic door alarm. (See *Appendix 1, Traveler Resources*, page 125).

- Do not open the door unless you know the identity or motive of the visitor. Phone the front desk clerk. Do not let strangers into your room. If your room has a peep hole, use it! If there is no peep hole, secure the chain lock, then open the door to verify identity.

---

***If a stranger knocks and says he's from the hotel staff, call the front desk to check before opening the door.***

---

- If you must open your door at night to an unverified person, turn off the lights in your room first. By doing so, you can clearly see the person, but he cannot see you.

- Keep your door locked when in your room and, if there's a chain lock, twist it to reduce slack before latching it.
- Avoid entering dark hallways or stairwells.
- Lock all doors and windows while showering or using the bathroom and hide your valuables and wallet.
- **Never** leave your room key in the outside key hole.
- If you lose your key, notify the desk and request another **room**—not another key.
- Do not tell the desk clerk that you are going out, or else the whole staff may know your room is vacant. Similarly, some hotels ask you to turn in your room key when you are going out. Don't!
- When out of your room you can fool a burglar into thinking that you're in your room by constructing a false chain lock, i.e., attach a short wire or bobby pin to a chain link, curve the end, then "hook" it in the chain track when you leave.

---

*To avoid fumbling for your key and wasting time making yourself a target, have your key in hand before reaching your door.*

---

- Some travelers use only those hotels that use the new plastic or cardboard keys instead of conventional metal keys (this combination system avoids the problem of loose keys to your room floating around).
- If a burglar gains entrance to your room at night while you're in bed, it is often safest to feign sleep.
- Keep an emergency light accessible, e.g., flashlight.
- Keep a low profile; if you have status and wealth don't flaunt it.
- If returning at night by taxi, ask the driver to wait until you are inside. If returning by public transportation, get off at the *nearest* stop.

**Additional considerations when staying in hotels abroad:**

- If you have reservations, obtain written confirmation so you don't get bumped if the hotel overbooks (a common practice).

- Carry the hotel's name and address with you in case you forget; these are often written on matches and stationery in your room.

- Once at your destination, tourist information offices often have room-finding services or can direct you to one. Some travel guides also list hotels with descriptions and telephone numbers.

- Many places in the world have uneven water pressure, limited hot water (and sometimes none), and sporadic electric power (and sometimes none).

- Ask the desk clerk when the best time to bathe or shower is, i.e., when it's most likely that you will have plenty of hot water.

- Pull back the covers to check for clean sheets and bed bugs (don't take anything for granted!).

- Many corridor lights are timed and only go on for short periods of time, therefore you could get caught in a dark hallway, so know your way around or carry a small flashlight.

- Be mentally prepared to leave whatever you have at any time; do not become attached to anything you have with you.

- Inquire of your lodging's staff about local traditions with which you should be aware, areas of town to avoid, times of day or night and even days of the week not to be out and about.

**Familiarize yourself with the general operations of the facility:**

- Is there an all night desk clerk?
- Are the outside entrances locked at night?
- Is there a security staff?
- Is the water drinkable?

- Is the facility located near transportation?
- Can you make international calls on their phones?
- Are the **hot** and **cold** faucets in their normal position?

## Motel/Hotel Fire

Preparing to survive in the event of a motel or hotel fire begins upon checking in. Survival is **your** responsibility; do not rely on the fire department to get you out in time. **Fire Prevention Bureaus** recommend the following fire safety tips:

- Select a room no higher than the second floor in case you need to jump to safety (jumpers almost never survive a third-story fall). Even though most fire departments have trucks with ladders that will reach above the second floor, they may not be able to get to the fire in time, or they may begin rescue efforts on a different side of the building, or they may not be able to get their truck to your side of the building, e.g., due to a narrow alley.
- Your lodging should have at least two means of egress in case of fire. Be sure that they are unlocked and unblocked.

---

*Count the number of doors from your room to the emergency exits so you can find them in the event of smoke in the hallway.*

---

- Check the smoke detector in your room by pushing the test button. If it does not work, request that it be fixed or get another room that has a functioning detector.
- For extra safety, pack a portable smoke alarm (obtainable in housewares stores).
- Pack a personal smoke hood (see *Appendix 1, Traveler Resources*, page 125).
- Learn the basic floor plan of your motel or hotel, note all fire exits, fire alarms, extinguishers, and means of egress (especially those closest to your room), and read the fire safety instructions in your room.

**In case of fire:**

- If you hear a fire alarm, **act**!

- Don't investigate, but report a fire or smoke immediately to the desk and fire department. **Remain calm!**

- If you spot a fire or see or smell smoke, pull a fire alarm and leave the building (most alarms are located near exits).

- Use stairways, **never** elevators. Elevator shafts can become chimneys for carrying smoke, and if the door opens and smoke enters, it blocks the light path of the automatic door. Properly designed stairwells are considered safe areas.

- Notify the front desk and fire department.

- Take your room key with you in case you are unable to exit the building and must return to your room (most self-lock upon closing).

- If you're in your room and hear an alarm or smell smoke, check the temperature of your door before exiting; if it's hot, don't open your door. If the door is cool, open it a crack, but be ready to close it fast.

- If the hallway is free of smoke and fire, walk quickly to the nearest exit alerting others on the floor. Close all doors behind you.

- If you leave your room and the smoke in the hallway is too thick to see (or it's dark), crawl with a wet towel over your face and count the doors by feel to the nearest emergency exit (this prevents you from getting lost so you can find your room if you need to return).

_____

*Before opening any door, including exit doors, feel for heat; if it's not hot, open slowly and observe for smoke and fire. If it's hot or you encounter smoke or fire, retreat and try a second exit.*

_____

- If you encounter smoke or fire at all exits, return to your room.

- If you can't leave your room, place wet towels, blankets, or curtains under the door and cover all vents and cracks to keep the smoke out. Thoroughly wet down everything by the doorway.

- Try to escape out the outside window.

- If confined to your room, keep the windows closed. If smoke gets in your room, breathe through a wet towel to protect your lungs and stay close to the floor.

- Shut off all fans, i.e., air conditioner, heater, bathroom vent, as they will probably draw in smoke or vent the fire.

- Fill the bathtub and use your ice bucket to put out flames.

- Call the desk and fire department and tell them that you are trapped in your room. Give them your room number.

- Hang a sheet out the window to call attention to your location and shut the window again.

## In the Elevator

Elevators and their corridors are ideal areas for crimes of opportunity, so be alert and observe the following precautions:

- Look up and down the corridors before boarding or deboarding.

- Check the interior of the elevator before entering. If occupied and doesn't feel safe, take the next one or the stairs.

- If you are alone and someone you have an uneasy feeling about or who looks suspicious is about to get on with you, don't get on. If it's too late, push the **door open** or **lobby** button and get off.

- Pay attention to your intuition. If you feel uneasy in an elevator (or stairwell or corridor) get out and go back to the lobby and start over or take a different route.

- On entering an elevator, move to the control panel and familiarize yourself with the controls (they differ from country to country).

- Only ride elevators going in your direction, e.g., if you are in the lobby and your destination is the 2nd floor, don't take an elevator going to the basement. To do so increases your time, hence exposure, on an elevator.

---

*If someone suspicious enters the elevator, get off.*
*Keep your hand on the door button.*

---

- If you are a woman alone and a man gets in with you and doesn't push a button, you know that he's going to get off on your floor. So, return to the lobby and take another elevator.
- If on a moving elevator and a passenger's behavior makes you suspicious, face them with your back to the control panel with your finger on the emergency button.

## Restrooms

Foreign restrooms are all too often just that—foreign to us in every way. Availability, quality, and levels of sanitation and privacy all vary tremendously. Some are used by both  sexes, others don't lock, others have little privacy, still others don't even have toilets, only holes in the floor. To help survive this frequent nemesis of travelers, follow these hints and precautions:

- Avoid unnecessary use of bathrooms by avoiding catching dysentery (see *Health & Medical Preparation* on page 13)!
- Depending on your destination, it may be wise to take your own supply of toilet paper. In many foreign countries the consistency may range from newspaper to sandpaper, if there's any at all.
- Bring along disposable toilet seat covers.
- Even finding a toilet may be a problem. Your best bet is a hotel, restaurant, museum or other public building.

- If you can't find the Restroom, look for the W.C. (*water closet*), or the male/female symbol. W.C.s are usually for both sexes.

- Use public restrooms with caution; have someone with you.

- Women should beware of female purse-snatchers in restrooms.

- If you take off your jewelry to wash, put it in your pocket, not on the sink or shelf!

- Matches may be a blessing to help alleviate the odor.

## On the Phone

If you have never appreciated Ma Bell, you will when you return from a trip out of the country. Phones are often difficult to find, the service can be poor, and you can expect long waits for the operator, language barriers, difficulty in getting connections (which often prove to be poor connections), and frequent disconnects. To help not being a target on the phone:

- Learn the locations of phones in the area you're visiting.

- The best place to find phones will usually be airports, train stations, hotels, and government buildings.

- Before selecting a phone booth or station, scan the immediate environment and assess its safety.

- The best place to make a long distance call is usually the central post office which has no surcharges. This is also true for some train stations and airports — check first. Place your call at odd hours as these phones may have waiting lines.

- Ask about surcharges before placing your call; **they can be as much as 400% over the cost of the call!**

- Hotels may add their own surcharges if calling from your room.

- Many countries honor U.S. calling cards and they often qualify you for reduced surcharges.

- Memorize your credit card calling numbers. Before dialing the numbers, look around to be sure no one is watching close by. As an extra precaution stand in such a way as to block others view of the number pad. If you must refer to your calling card, hold it discreetly in your hand and put it away promptly.

- Public telephones in some countries handle international calls, but don't bet on it. To find a phone on which you can place an international call, go to a hotel that caters to foreigners.

- Before leaving on your trip, you can check with the phone company for international calling procedures.

---

*When talking on a public phone, turn your back to the dial so that you can observe any activity around you.*

---

- Don't leave your luggage unattended to make a call. Either secure it first or take it with you.

- Have emergency numbers accessible, e.g., for the local police, the U.S. Consulate. Emergency numbers are usually listed in the front of telephone books worldwide.

- Find out what type of coins or tokens public phones take; they are available at newsstands, bars, or wherever there are public phones.

## Mail

- Leave your itinerary and mailing addresses with family and friends who may need to write.

- Letters sent to you should have Hold for Arrival and your arrival date written on the envelope.

- Mail should only be sent airmail with at least a week allowed for delivery.

- Mail can be sent to your hotel, in care of the American Express office, or to general delivery (Poste Restante, French; Postlagernde Sendungen, German; Posta Restante, Italian; Fermo Posta, Spanish). U.S. Embassies and Consulates do not handle private mail.

- When writing home, aerograms are the least expensive and fastest means. Buy them at the post office.

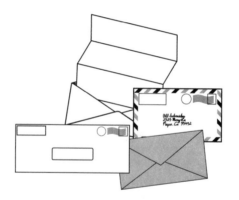

# Law and Order

## Authorities & the Law

There has been an increase in the number of Americans arrested, detained, or *in trouble* while traveling. Most travelers are charged for minor infractions, but some are charged with serious crimes, e.g., drug charges, smuggling or espionage. Most violations concern improper documents, unknowingly violating local statutes, fraud, currency violations, and vehicle violations. To avoid getting into trouble, and knowing what to do if you do get into trouble, observe the following:

- Know the "rules" and general customs of the culture.

- Familiarize yourself with the laws and methods of local law enforcement, e.g., many foreign police forces operate on a graft system, and you are expected to pay to **stay** out of trouble, or to **get** out of trouble. Know before you go.

---

*When in different countries you are subject to their laws, and their system of justice may be entirely different from ours. There may be unlimited detention without probable cause or arrest, and the Bill of Rights has never been heard of.*

---

- Immigration violations usually include improper papers (i.e., passport or visa) or falsifying reasons for entering the country.

- Customs violations usually involve the illegal removal of restricted objects from the country. One lady unknowingly purchased a valuable vase, an 800-year-old archaeological treasure; she spent a year in jail.

- In some countries, it is normal procedure required by law

for you to leave your passport at the hotel desk overnight so it can be checked by local police. In other countries, you may be required to fill out a **police card** listing your name, passport number, destination, local address, and reason for traveling.

- You cannot remove currency from some countries and currency limits are regulated in others. Ask.
- A few countries require that you have enough money for your trip and/or your ongoing or return tickets.
- Be prepared to pay a **departure tax** before boarding your return flight in some countries, e.g., the Bahamas.
- The mere possession of alcohol in Moslem countries can bring a sentence of 5 years and 80 lashes.

---

*Don't drink and drive. Even one drink can land you in jail for three weeks in some countries like Austria, Denmark, Finland, Norway, and Sweden.*

---

- If stopped for speeding or other moving violations, you can often pay your fine on the spot.
- If you cause a serious accident, you may face criminal charges.
- Road permits in lieu of tolls for divided highways are required in certain countries, e.g., Switzerland. Driving on these highways without a permit is a fineable offense. Check with the Consulate before driving to see if these permits are required.
- Don't sell any personal items such as jewelry or clothing. This is against the law in some countries and the penalties are severe.
- Illegal trafficking in drugs, even small amounts, across borders is a major offense. Some countries make no distinction between hard and soft drugs or between possession of small amounts and drug trafficking. So, do not even think

about using or buying illegal drugs even for personal use.

- Do not enter restricted areas.

- Familiarize yourself with uniforms, insignias, and emblems that denote rank or authority.

- Be alert to persons who may be disguised as officers or officials. If stopped by a law enforcement officer, ask to see his ID card. If he can't produce one he's probably an imposter, even if he shows you a badge (the badge means nothing as they are easily obtained through mail-order houses and illicit outlets).

- Don't argue with the law, even if you think they are wrong.

- In Eastern Bloc and some Third World countries, discussing politics could be hazardous, i.e., even a seemingly innocent statement may be construed as anti-state agitation.

---

*Never deliver packages for anyone*
*unless you are certain they do not*
*contain drugs or other contraband.*

---

## If Arrested

If arrested, you will be subject to the legal procedures of that country (which may differ substantially from what you're accustomed to), and the Consulate will be unable to obtain favored treatment for you. You can assume that you are in serious trouble. Few countries provide a jury trial, most don't accept bail, and pretrial detention in solitary may last months. Prisons often are very inhumane with inadequate diet, and without even minimal comforts or essentials. Physical abuse is not uncommon and the guards and officials may not speak English.

- If arrested, notify the American Consulate as soon as possible, who will provide you with a list of English-speaking attorneys, notify your family, and monitor your detention conditions and treatment. It is not within the mandate of the Consulate to represent you.

- Don't expect the Marines or that the American Consulate will "get you off". They may not even have the time to actively assist you.

## Traveling in High-Risk Areas Abroad

The Department of State issues *Travel Advisories and Warnings* regarding travel to specific countries or areas (see *Appendix 1, Traveler Resources,* page 125). The **Bureau of Consular Affairs** makes the following recommendations if you must travel in an area with a history of terrorist incidences or kidnapping:

**DANGER**

- Make sure your affairs are in order before you leave home and discuss with your family what to do in case of an emergency.

- When you arrive at your destination, register with the U.S. Embassy or Consulate (which you should also do if traveling in Eastern Europe or Russia). This makes it easier for the Consul to help you if you encounter difficulty, and aids contacting you in case of emergency.

- If you are planning to visit a country where there is no U.S. Embassy or Consulate (e.g., Albania and South Yemen), register in an adjacent country, leave your itinerary, and inquire about the conditions in your target country.

- Be cautious about discussing you itinerary, business, or personal matters.

- Avoid "flagship" hotels that are frequented by the wealthy, businessmen, and diplomats. They are popular terrorist targets. Choose smaller local hotels instead. Similarly, it's best to stay away from embassies and consulates.

- Avoid wearing "power" clothes and military haircuts; you don't want to be mistaken for a rich American, diplomat, or military person.

- Don't leave any personal or business papers in your hotel room.

---

*Watch for people following you or "loiterers" observing your comings and goings.*

---

- Avoid predictable times, modes, and routes of travel. Vary your routines.
- Select your own taxicabs at random (use your intuition or gut feeling), and be sure it is a legitimate cab, i.e., don't take a cab which is not clearly identified as a taxi. Compare the face of the driver with the one posted on his license.
- Note the location of safe havens, e.g., police stations, hotels, fire stations, hospitals, public buildings.
- It is best to travel with a companion. Keep him informed of your plans and whereabouts if you must go out alone.
- Be certain of the identity of visitors to your hotel room before opening the door. It's best to meet visitors in the lobby.
- Don't meet strangers at unknown or remote locations.
- Refuse unexpected packages.
- Carefully check your car (see *Executive Safety* on page 39).
- Be sure your vehicle is in good operating condition in case you need to resort to high-speed or evasive driving.
- Drive with windows closed on crowded streets so bombs can't be thrown in your car. Keep doors locked and **drive strategically** (see *Driving at Home and Abroad* on page 77).
- Constantly formulate plans of action in case of danger.
- If you are ever in a situation where there's shooting, drop to the floor and don't move until the danger has passed. Shield yourself behind or under a solid object if possible. If you must move, crawl!

- Should a civil or political disturbance, war, or terrorist incident occur while traveling in a foreign country, stay clear of the action, contact the Consulate, and notify your family that you are safe.

- While staying in a high-risk area, keep current of local affairs by reading the newspaper and listening to the radio.

- When traveling through high-risk areas by air, pay particular obeisance to the safety tips in *At the Airport* on page 65, as airports are favorite places for terrorists. In addition, avoid sitting near the gate where your plane departs until you hear the boarding announcement. Once on board, give your seat a security check, i.e., look under the seat, in the overhead bin, and in the seat pocket for packages or wires. Pick your seat strategically (see *Executive Safety* on page 39).

## Terrorism

The chances of ever becoming involved in a terrorist incident are extremely remote. Due to their random and unpredictable nature, it is impossible to avoid the possibility entirely; it's usually a matter of simply being in the wrong place at the wrong time. A major objective of most terrorists is to take hostages as bargaining chips. A convenient source of hostages has proven to be the airplane. If you ever become a hostage, the odds are overwhelmingly in favor of eventual release, and you are a valuable commodity to your captors, so it's generally in their interests to keep you alive. There are no hard and fast rules, but in the event of becoming a hostage, the following recommendations taken from a number of experts will help keep you safe:

- Do not resist, obey instructions, and provide only the information asked for. Forget about being a hero. Attempt escape only if there is a good probability of succeeding.

- Follow any instructions from the flight crew; most international carriers train their crews on how to respond to a hijacking.

- Every attempt will be made by your captors to intimidate you through physical and mental abuse.

118

- Don't make any sudden moves as they may be miscon-strued by a nervous and trigger-happy terrorist.

- Stay calm (fear can be as dangerous as any attacker), cooperate, and try not to provoke your captors. Don't display authority, arrogance or disdain, and don't argue. You start shouting, they start hitting.

- Take inventory of your situation and weigh your alterna-tives. Constantly think and observe.

*Refrain from talking to other passengers. If you must, do so in a normal voice; don't whisper as it may be misconstrued as plotting.*

- Try to establish good communications with those of your captors who seem receptive, but don't offer suggestions, make promises, or ask for special privileges, e.g., smoking. Don't try to reason with them.

- Ask permission for everything, e.g., use of the lavatory, getting a drink, moving about.

- Since you may not be allowed to use the lavatory, drink few liquids. It is normal to experience a loss of appetite and weight.

- Wear as much clothing as possible (even if overly warm) as it will provide some additional protection from shrapnel in case of a blast.

- Keep the floor area in front of your seat clear so you have a space to take cover if shooting starts. Use a blanket, jacket, or pillow to cover you for some added protection.

- Do not provide any information that may be useful to your captors.

- Accept captivity with hope and confidence and try to keep your spirits up. Prepare yourself mentally and emotionally for what may be a long and stressful ordeal.

- Keep your sense of humor and dignity. Never grovel or beg.

- Try to gain the respect of your captors.

- Avoid discussing politics or religion, and avoid prolonged eye contact. Be inconspicuous.

- Save your strength, try to exercise, eat regularly, and keep clean and comfortable.

---

*Guard against the "Stockholm Syndrome" in which the captive forms a strong attachment to the captors.*

---

- Try to constructively pass time. Play mental "what if?" games, e.g., what if there is a rescue attempt?

- If possible move towards an exit and away from the aisle; the passengers in aisle seats are most subject to gunfire and abuse.

- Learn how to open the emergency exits by reading the information card when you have a chance.

- Stay alert and prepared to respond quickly to any change in your situation. Know when to cooperate, but also when to take action.
- Be observant and make mental notes of your captors' behavior.
- In the event of gunfire, dive for any available cover and stay down until certain that it is safe to move.
- If your captors are particularly hostile to your country (e.g., Americans traveling in Iran), and if the flight attendants are instructed to collect passports, ask her (if you can) to either not take yours or hide it.
- In the event of a rescue attempt, try to stay out of the line of fire and be ready to make a break for safety to avoid being caught in a crossfire or last minute execution.
- Don't attempt to help rescuers or pick up a weapon.
- For the safest seating locations, see *Executive Safety*, page 39.

## If Destitute, Ill, or Injured

- Should you run out of money while abroad, contact the American Consul who will help you get in touch with your family, bank, or employer, and tell you how to arrange for them to send you money (see *The Consulate: When You Need Help* below). The Consulate **cannot** lend you money. Never use your passport as collateral for a loan.
- If you become seriously ill or injured while traveling abroad, contact the American Consul who will help you find medical assistance and inform your family or friends.
- Implement contingency plans.

## The Consulate: When You Need Help

Traveling on an American passport will get you out of trouble, warrant special treatment from local officials, and get you off if arrested. Right? **Wrong!** The U.S. Consulate, whose function is to help Americans in trouble, can get you out of jail, give you legal

advice, plan your trip, cash your checks, or lend you money. Right? **Wrong!**

Americans traveling in any foreign country are subject to the laws of that country; ignorance is no excuse. Due to legal and budgetary constraints and excessive work loads, the American Consulate cannot be all things to all people. Its function is only to *assist* you if in trouble, not to *solve* your problem. The Consulate must work within the local laws, statutes, and regulations.

- There are more than 250 U.S. Embassies and Consulates worldwide. *Key Officers of Foreign Service Posts* provides names of key officers and addresses for all U.S. Embassies and Consulates abroad.

- **The Citizens Services Section of the Consulate can help you by providing the following information and assistance:**

  - A listing of English-speaking attorneys and doctors.
  - Help you contact family and friends if arrested or hospitalized.
  - Aid in replacing your passport if lost or stolen.
  - Issue travel advisories.
  - Notarize documents.
  - Tell you how to obtain foreign public documents.
  - May provide helpful information if you have a legal problem.
  - Facilitate the transmission of funds to you from family or friends, i.e., an individual in the States can send a money

order or wire money to the State Department's account at American Security Bank, State Department Branch 20, Washington, D.C. 20520, along with your name and address and the name of the receiver and the American Embassy or Consulate to which it should be sent (fees will be charged for this service).

- If you are concerned about an American in trouble abroad, contact the **Overseas Citizens Services.**

## Immigration & Customs

When returning to this country, you must go through an Immigration and Customs check. The Immigration check simply involves a brief interview with an official whose duty it is to determine if the passport is valid (i.e., checking the expiration date and for signs of tampering) and that the holder is the person identified in the passport.

After Immigration you go through Customs. It is the traveler's obligation to declare all imported goods which may be subject to duty beyond the general personal exemption.

- For detailed information about Customs, including regulations, procedures, and duty rates, write for the brochure, *Know Before You Go, Customs Hints for Returning Residents*, from the **U.S. Customs Service**.

- Have all your documents handy, i.e., passport, a *certificate of registration*, *International Certificate of Vaccination*, and all receipts.

- For the purpose of assessing duty, all goods purchased out-of-country are valued at their actual purchase price. Therefore, keep all purchase receipts.

- A *Customs Declaration* form must be completed before passing through Customs (families can submit a single joint form).

---

***Duty is due in full upon arrival in this country.***

---

- You must pay duty on items purchased abroad and mailed home.

- You can mail **gifts** home from abroad without duty if the value of each gift does not exceed the current specified amount.

- If you mail items home that you purchased in the U.S., mark the package *American goods returned*. There will be no duty.

- Most meat, fruit, vegetables, plants, animal products, furs and pelts from endangered species, items made from sea turtle shell and crocodile leather, and many species of live animals will be impounded.

- Pack items to be declared separately for ease of inspection.

- Dress neatly and take time to be well-groomed in order to avoid looking suspicious.

---

*Just as it is not nice to try and fool Mother Nature, don't try to fool a Customs agent.*

---

# *Appendix 1*

## Traveler Resources

In addition to the numerous resources for travel information referenced through out **TRAVEL SAFELY**, the following businesses and organizations are listed as some of the reliable sources available to the prepared traveler.

### Travel Accessories Catalogues

For a wide selection of inovative hard-to-find travel safety products and accessories, e.g., travel locks and alarms, money belts and pouches, voltage converters and plug adapters, portable electric personal applicances, lead lined film pouches, international travel clocks, money exchange calculators, water purifiers/filters, travel health kits, language translators, emergency escape smoke hood and more:

**Magellan's**
P.O. Box 5485
Santa Barbara, CA 93150
1-800-962-4943
FAX 1-805-568-5406

**Traveler's Checklist**
Cornwall Bridge Road
336 Sharon, CT 06069
1-800-842-3064
FAX 1-860-364-0369

### Travel Information

**World Status:** a computer disk program that contains vital travel information from 230 countries and principalities, e.g., medical/vaccination information, passport/visa requirements, State Dept. advisories, analyst commentary on political conditions, currency/exchange rate.

**Pinkerton World Status Map:** A pocket-sized world map, issued bi-monthly presenting health and safety information for the world traveler, e.g. risk levels for problem countries with corresponding summaries of U.S. State Department travel advisories.

**Pinkerton Eye on Travel**
200 North Glebe Rd., Suite 1011
Arlington, VA 22203-3728
To order a free disk/map: (703) 525-6111

## Security Education and Information

Instruction and consultation in travel safety, security, threat identification and avoidance of terrorism and crime. Country analysis reports and customized consultations for employees of government agencies, private corporations and individuals.

> **Mayer Nudell**
> 210 E. Fairfax St., #211
> Falls Church, VA 22046-2906
> (703) 237-2513
> FAX 1-703 533-0358
> Internet: MNudell@AOL•com

## Airline Passenger Safety

Programs and products for personal or corporate airline passenger safety training:

> **SAFEAIR Services, Inc.**
> 4827 West Royal Lane, Suite A
> Irving, TX 75063
> 1-800-388-1821

## Aviation Safety

For a current evaluation of airline travel, from a non-profit organization, aligned to no interest group, acting as consumer advocate for enhanced aviation safety:

> **Aviation Safety Institue (ASI)**
> 6797 N. High, Suite 316
> Worthington, OH 43085
> (614) 885-4242
> Compuserv or Internet: AVSIG

## Self Defense

A professional self-defense and personal empowerment class for women, children, teens and men. This is a full contact self-defense training, not a martial art. Training available nationwide:

**IMPACT Personal Safety**
1-800-345-KICK (1-800-345-5425)


## Government Advisories

U.S. State Department: **Citizens Emergency Center**
(202) 647-5225 (Touch-tone phone only)

**Centers for Disease Control**
Atlanta, GA 30333
(404) 332-4559


## International Medical Assistance

**International Association for Medical Assistance to Travelers (IAMAT)**
417 Center St.
Lewiston, NY 14092
(716) 754-4883

**MedEscort International**
P.O. Box 8766
Allentown, PA 18105-8766
1-800-255-7182

**Medic Alert emblem**
2323 Colorado Ave.
Turlock, CA 95382
1-800-344-3226

**Traveling Nurse's Network**
P.O. Box 129
Vancouver, WA 98666
(360) 694-2462

**International SOS Assistance**
P.O. Box 11568
Philadelphia, PA 19116
1-800-523-8930

## Specialized Travel Groups

**Travel Companion Exchange, Inc.**
P.O. Box 833
Amityville, NY 11701
(516) 454-0880

**Youth for Understanding**
3501 Newark St. N.W.
Washington, D.C. 20016
1-800-TEE-NAGE (833-6243)

**American Youth Hostels**
733 15th St. N.W., Suite 840
Washington, D.C. 20005
(202) 783-6161

**Elderhostel**
75 Federal Street
Boston, MA 02116
(617) 426-7788

**Grand Circle Travel**
347 Cougress Street
Boston, MA 02210
1-800-221-2610

## Associations

**International Airline Passengers Association (IAPA)**
P.O. Box 870188
Dallas TX 75387-0188
1-800-821-4272

**American Automobile Association (AAA)**
Contact your local AAA office.
Emergency Road Service for members:
1-800-AAA-HELP  (1-800-222-4357)

**American Association of Retired Persons (AARP)**
601 E. Street, N.W.
Washington, D.C. 20049
(202) 434-2277

**Society for the Advancement of Travel for the Handicapped (SATH)**
347 Fifth Ave., Suite 610
New York, NY 10016
(212) 447-7284

# *Appendix 2*

## International Vocabulary of Safety

| English | Italian | German | Spanish | French |
|---|---|---|---|---|
| Police | Polizia | Polizei | Policia | Police |
| Help! | Aiuto! | Hilfe! | Socorro! | Au secours! |
| Fire! | Fuoco! | Feuer! | Fuego! | Feu! |
| Doctor | Medico | Arzt | Medico | Docteur |
| hospital | ospedale | krankenhaus | hospital | hopital |
| pain | dolore | die pein | dolor | douleur |
| sick | malato | mir ist schlecht | malo infermo | enfermo |
| I'm lost. | Mi sono perso. | Ich habe mich verirrt. | Me he perdido. | Je me suis perdu. |
| I'm hungry. | Ho fame. | Ich habe hunger. | Tengo hambre. | J'ai faim. |
| I'm thirsty. | Ho sete. | Ich habe durst. | Tengo sed. | J'ai soif. |
| Hello. | Buon giorno. | Guten tag. | Buenos dias. | Bonjour. |
| Yes. | Si. | Ja. | Si. | Oui. |
| No. | No. | Nein. | No. | Non. |
| Please. | Per piacere. | Bitte. | Por favor. | S'il vous plait. |
| Thank you. | Grazie. | Danke. | Gracias. | Merci. |
| Do you speak English? | Parla Inglese? | Sprechen sie Englisch? | Habla usted Ingles? | Parlez-vous Anglais? |
| toilet | gabinetto | toilette | lavabo | toilettes |
| telephone | telefono | telephon | telefono | tele'phone |

# *Appendix 3*

## Universal Signs

Throughout the world there are some 5,000 languages and dialects in use today. This necessitates a visual international language of signs, made up of symbols and colors, to accommodate the world traveler. Four basic symbols are used to indicate:

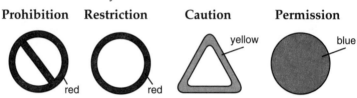

Take the symbol for prohibition and apply it to any activity and you prohibit that activity:

The United Nations has adopted the use of color for instant recognition and emphasis:

**RED** = prohibition          **YELLOW/ORANGE** = caution

**GREEN** = safe               **BLUE** = permission/access

**BROWN** = recreation          **PURPLE** = radiation hazard

Although not yet standardized, three dimensional shapes serve as tough symbols. You must take a few minutes to familiarize yourself with the ones used in any particular application, e.g., your foreign rented car. Their most important aspect is that they can be recognized by touch instead of sight. These shapes are usually a variation of some form such as:

The following page shows some of the more common international symbols related to safety.

| | | | |
|---|---|---|---|
| flight information | baggage check-in | passenger check-in | baggage claim |
| customs | information | baggage locker | toilets |
| lodging | dining | handicap | pedestrian crossing |
| no entry | railroad | two-way | no passing |
| camping | drinking water | filling station | hospital |
| telephone | bioharzard infectous | radioactive | civil defense |

# *Appendix 4*

## Metric Conversion Table
### Common Equivalents and Conversions

| Customary to Metric | Metric to Customary |
|---|---|

**LENGTH**

| | | | |
|---|---|---|---|
| 1 inch | = 2.5 centimeters | 1 millimeter | =.04 inch |
| 1 foot | = 0.3 meter | 1 meter | = 3.3 feet |
| 1 yard | = 0.9 meter | 1 meter | = 1.1 yards |
| 1 mile | = 1.6 kilometers | 1 kilometer | = 0.6 mile |

**LIQUID VOLUME**

| | | | |
|---|---|---|---|
| 1 ounce | = 30 milliliters | 1 milliliter | = .034 ounce |
| 1 pint | = .47 liter | 1 liter | = 2.1 pints |
| 1 quart | = .95 liter | 1 liter | = 1.05 quarts |
| 1 gallon | = 3.8 liters | 1 liter | = .26 gallon |

**MASS**

| | | | |
|---|---|---|---|
| 1 ounce | = 28 grams | 1 gram | = .035 ounce |
| 1 pound | = .45 kilogram | 1 kilogram | = 2.2 pounds |

**AREA**

| | | | |
|---|---|---|---|
| 1 sq. inch | = 6.5 sq. centimeters | 1 sq. cm. | = .16 sq. inch |
| 1 sq. foot | = .09 sq. meter | 1 sq. meter | = 11 sq. feet |
| 1 sq. yard | = .8 sq. meter | 1 sq. meter | = 1.2 sq. yds. |
| 1 sq. mile | = 2.6 sq. kilometers | 1 sq. km | = .4 sq. mile |

**MILES INTO KILOMETERS**

| miles | 10 | 20 | 30 | 40 | 50 | 60 | 70 | 80 | 90 | 100 |
|---|---|---|---|---|---|---|---|---|---|---|
| km | 16 | 32 | 48 | 64 | 80 | 97 | 113 | 129 | 145 | 161 |

**KILOMETERS INTO MILES**

| km | 10 | 20 | 30 | 40 | 50 | 60 | 70 | 80 | 90 | 100 | 110 |
|---|---|---|---|---|---|---|---|---|---|---|---|
| miles | 6 | 12 | 19 | 25 | 31 | 37 | 44 | 50 | 56 | 62 | 68 |

**TEMPERATURE**

Celsius = 5/9 (°F - 32)
Fahrenheit = 9/5 °C + 32

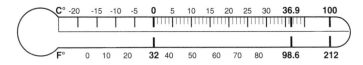

# *Appendix 5*

## Pretravel Information for the Family

Your spouse, attorney, trustee, a family member, relative or trusted friend should know the location of the following documents and information:

- ❏ Passport duplicate information
- ❏ Itinerary of trip
- ❏ Last Will and Testament
- ❏ Living Will
- ❏ Birth Certificate
- ❏ Marriage License
- ❏ Divorce Records
- ❏ Deeds
- ❏ Car Titles
- ❏ Bank Statements
- ❏ Tax Returns
- ❏ Credit Card Companies' numbers
- ❏ Medical Records
  - ❏ Physician
  - ❏ Dentist
  - ❏ Blood type, drug allergies, etc.
- ❏ Social Security Number

- ❏ Power of Attorney
- ❏ Safety Deposit Box
  - ❏ location of key
- ❏ Keys and location to storage areas
- ❏ Attorney's name and number
- ❏ Accountant's name and number
- ❏ Military Discharge papers
- ❏ Stocks and Bonds
- ❏ Insurance Policies
  - ❏ Life
  - ❏ Health
  - ❏ Accident
  - ❏ Homeowners
  - ❏ Car
- ❏ Trusts
- ❏ VA Benefits
- ❏ Funeral Arrangements

If you are concerned about a family member abroad contact:

**The Department of States Overseas Citizen's Services**
(202) 647-9081

In case a family member needs emergency funds transfer the money through:

**American Security Bank**
State Department Account, Branch 20
Washington, D.C. 20520

# Index

To order additional copies of

# *Travel Safely*

### AT HOME AND ABROAD

contact:

**Uniquest Publications (406) 443-3911**
**562 West Main • Helena, MT 59601**
for corporate sales and
custom imprinting.

## OR

Contact:
**Falcon Press Publishing, Co.**
**call toll-free**
**1-800-582-2665**
for **all** other purchases.

## ORDER TODAY!